The Evolution Angel

The Evolution Angel

An Emergency Physician's
Lessons with Death and the Divine

TODD MICHAEL

JEREMY P. TARCHER/PENGUIN
a member of Penguin Group (USA) Inc.
New York

JEREMY P. TARCHER/PENGUIN
Published by the Penguin Group
Penguin Group (USA) Inc., 375 Hudson Street, New York, New York 10014, USA • Penguin
Group (Canada), 90 Eglinton Avenue East, Suite 700, Toronto, Ontario M4P 2Y3, Canada
(a division of Pearson Canada Inc.) • Penguin Books Ltd, 80 Strand, London WC2R 0RL,
England • Penguin Ireland, 25 St Stephen's Green, Dublin 2, Ireland (a division of Penguin
Books Ltd) • Penguin Group (Australia), 250 Camberwell Road, Camberwell, Victoria 3124,
Australia (a division of Pearson Australia Group Pty Ltd) • Penguin Books India Pvt Ltd,
11 Community Centre, Panchsheel Park, New Delhi–110 017, India • Penguin Group (NZ),
67 Apollo Drive, Rosedale, North Shore 0632, New Zealand (a division of Pearson
New Zealand Ltd) • Penguin Books (South Africa) (Pty) Ltd, 24 Sturdee Avenue,
Rosebank, Johannesburg 2196, South Africa

Penguin Books Ltd, Registered Offices: 80 Strand, London WC2R 0RL, England

Most Tarcher/Penguin books are available at special quantity discounts for bulk purchase for sales promotions,
premiums, fund-raising, and educational needs. Special books or book excerpts also can be created to fit specific
needs. For details, write Penguin Group (USA) Inc. Special Markets, 375 Hudson Street, New York, NY 10014.

Library of Congress Cataloging-in-Publication Data
Michael, Todd, date.
The evolution angel : an emergency physician's lessons
with death and the divine / Todd Michael.
p.   cm.
ISBN 978-1-58542-671-3
1. Michael, Todd, date. 2. Mediums—Biography. 3. Spiritualism. 4. Angels.
5. Emergency medicine—Miscellanea. I. Title.
BF1283.M53A3   2008   2008018355
133.9—dc22

Printed in the United States of America
1 3 5 7 9 10 8 6 4 2

BOOK DESIGN BY NICOLE LAROCHE

For Julian

That in your time
you will also know.

The Evolution Angel

Introduction

A line of towering thunderheads flickered in and out of view with each stroke of lightning. The road was covered with a treacherous sheen of water. It was nearly four in the morning and I had no business driving this late. Making matters worse, I had worked all night and I was dead tired. But I kept going. More than anything I wanted to make it home. In my fatigue I had neglected to fasten my seat belt.

The miles rolled by in the darkness and the rain poured down in sheets. My head began to nod but over and over I wrenched my attention back to the road. I struggled to stay awake, trying every trick I knew. I slapped myself on the cheeks. I shook my head. I sang. I chewed gum and I kept going, contemplating my most unsuccessful life. I was the piano player in a rock band and really nothing more than a garden-variety desperado. Although I thought I knew what I was doing at a conscious level, deep down I also knew perfectly well that I had no clue whatever as to what I was doing or where I was going. Deep down I was desperate for guidance and praying for a light in the darkness to appear.

Soon my mind began to drift and a parade of captivating images floated before me. I saw myself swinging back and forth on the swing set at my old grade school. Back and forth. Back and forth. And then I was gliding down, deeper and deeper into the well of memory, falling effortlessly, drinking in the feeling of deep relaxation that comes only with deep sleep.

The next thing I knew, a pair of soft hands grasped my face and pulled my head up sharply. A loud voice, kind but very firm, exploded in my head: "Wake up, Todd. Now." My eyes flew open and adrenaline surged through my solar plexus like a powerful electric shock. The car was hurtling directly toward a massive bridge abutment only fifty feet before me, the speedometer hovering near eighty. In a heartbeat, I wrenched the wheel to the left and a split second later the concrete pillar flashed by my right window.

I pulled over to the side of the road, shaken and gasping for breath. Physically and emotionally exhausted, I soon fell into a troubled sleep. Like the image of the deadly bridge abutment flashing past my window, images of my life began to race by in rapid succession. As though I were falling from a precipice to my death, I saw my entire life unravel sequentially before my eyes.

What I saw shook me. I watched myself experiencing a fair number of good moments as my life swept by, but there was something about the sum total of the experience that was disturbing and sorrowful. I hadn't really done anything that was all that bad or experienced anything inordinately traumatic. It wasn't that. It was what I *hadn't* done that really bothered me. I saw that I had spent the precious gift of life, the lavish series of stunning opportunities this fascinating world provides, just "getting by." I saw that I had been rather self-centered and had done relatively little to help anyone but myself. I had spent my life in survival mode, just trying to huddle up to whatever small fire I could find in the wilderness night. In scene after fleeting scene, I saw myself groping in the dark, feeling my way through blind alleys and dead-end pathways one after another after another. And then there was nothing. The next thing I knew, sunlight was pouring over the dashboard.

Clearly, something unusual had happened to me. Part of me entertained the possibility that perhaps a messenger or "angel" of some sort had awakened me before I struck the bridge. But my rational mind quickly rejected that possibility as a bunch of weak-minded, woo-woo nonsense. Surely it was all in my head—only my imagination, I told myself. I wanted very much to shake the frightening experience off and forget about it as quickly as possible.

But that would prove impossible. The experience, it would seem, was far from over: Things *kept* happening. For the next forty days, I experienced the most intense and profound series of changes I have ever known. My entire life was dismantled steadily, piece by piece, in an eerily "systematic" manner. I lost my job. A woman I loved more than life itself vanished from my life forever. My car died. My closest confidant moved away. My savings ran out. Finally, on exactly the fortieth day, in early February, in a typical thirty-below wind-chill Alberta Clipper, a faulty wood stove burned my cabin in the stark Iowa countryside to the ground, along with all my possessions. My insurance had lapsed and I was suddenly rendered homeless and penniless.

I hate when that happens.

My best friend, Ron, generously allowed me to sleep on the concrete floor in his basement—an act of kindness I will not forget. He even let me put in a plywood floor to ease the pain. There, with a few books, a set of oil paints, and a tiny black-and-white TV with three stations, I was left rudderless in a state of profound despair as a bitter northern winter howled at my tiny frost-encrusted window well. Times were bad, the winter was one blizzard after another, and work was scarce. I spent the bulk of my days huddled in a sleeping bag on the floor searching my mind for answers that never seemed to come. Over and over I prayed for guidance, but I felt totally alone—as though my prayers were nothing but leaves in the wind. Even God, it seemed, had vanished from the horizon.

Then something happened. Awakening one night from a series of vivid dreams, I felt as though someone or something had been speaking to me. But as powerful as the sensation was, I could remember nothing. Lying in the darkness, I then experienced a great, albeit outlandish, epiphany: Although I lacked any appropriate academic background—I had been majoring in that most lucrative of majors, philosophy, and had dropped out a number of years previously—I resolved to go back to college and do the unthinkable. I would obtain the requisite premedical credentials—straight A's in a rigorous curriculum of chemistry, physics, and biology, coupled with a famously wicked admissions test—and then go on to medical school. I would become a physician and devote my life to saving others' lives and easing their suffering.

Oh sure. You bet. No problem. Although that sounded noble enough on the surface, my friends and family understandably thought this plan utterly absurd. Had you known me then you would have readily agreed. At that point, my chances of succeeding at an eight-year gauntlet of grueling scientific and emotional initiations were laughable at best. In very literal terms, only a miracle—or at the very least a miraculous *transformation*—would allow me to succeed.

. . .

It would be seven years before I would hear any sort of "other-worldly" message again. When I did, it would be because of Matthew Slater's demise. I met Matthew the month I graduated from medical school. Premed, graduate school, and medical school were behind me. My wife, Lora, and I were looking for a place to live in the country near the hospital where I would intern. We needed a large garden space and the Slaters had just the thing—a ten-acre tract of fertile land complete with a two-acre garden plot. The area was famous for its melons, which grow in a certain type of deep, sandy soil.

Matthew was a brilliant pediatric cardiologist and intensivist. He had personally developed an intensive care unit that was known for hundreds of miles around. When a child was so gravely ill that no one else could help, he or she was flown to Matthew's unit as a very last resort. His dedication was such that he would often set up a cot next to patients undergoing the most critical phases of treatment and sleep next to them through the night until they had stabilized. He had saved many hopeless cases and had won the admiration of countless grateful parents and referring physicians. He was one of the most important and most beloved mentors I have known.

Matthew was a man of infinite kindness and patience. He was soft-spoken and naturally benign in that most comfortable of ways. His greatest pleasure was his gardening. He specialized in canta-loupes. The two of us split the garden half and half and I devoted my portion to my own specialty, watermelons. And let me tell you, we grew a lot of particularly nice melons in that sandy loam. The vines were huge and a thing of beauty in and of themselves.

We often met in the garden in the evenings after a particularly stressful shift and told each other of the day's trials and tribulations. He would listen to the hideous stuff that was happening for me and then manage to say something really brief, really calm—something that would inexplicably melt the entire situation away for me. I know now that this is how the truly wise often speak. But mostly Matthew just sat in the dusk in the middle of his lush field of melons with a faraway gaze. He seemed to savor every single minute of every day—and in the most intense way I have ever observed. At the end of the fall, he confided in me that two years ago he had been diagnosed with chronic leukemia.

That bitter Michigan winter was without a doubt the hardest of my entire life. The internship worked us routinely in thirty-six-hour continuous shifts. Sometimes we would be off a mere twelve hours and put right back on again for another thirty-six hours. The reports you hear about this are quite true. I wasn't very good at it, if truth be told. Although my teachers tried, I had all kinds of problems learning medicine and adjusting to the sterile military routine of a hospital. I was a philosopher, dammit, an *artist*. My peers occasionally thought me hopeless, I'm sure. But then again, most interns look hopeless at various points of time.

In due course, the hours and stress that had accumulated during the previous seven years and that peaked in thirty-six-hour-shift-land got to me. I fell gravely ill and was hospitalized for several weeks that frozen January. My recovery was tenuous and painful. In the middle of this, Matthew came down with pneumonia and, before anyone could even prepare themselves, died rapidly of respiratory failure one afternoon. He left a beautiful wife and a tiny daughter behind. I cannot speak of their grief, their hardship.

It was shortly thereafter that I heard the voice again. I had been praying and asking for guidance repeatedly. But once again, I was hearing nothing from God, sensing nothing at all. I began to feel abandoned and hopeless, languishing in an unrelenting agnostic haze. Then, lying awake one sleepless night, I felt a presence at the foot of the bed. I kept still. After a few minutes I heard a single word: "Write."

"Write? Write what? What are you talking about?" I queried. But there was no answer, as if to say, "You know." In a few moments the presence was gone.

That was many years ago. To this day, I shake my head in wonder when I look back upon the series of events that has driven me inexorably to this point. I see now that it all began that night when my life was saved by the hands and voice that deftly guided me from a certain and violent death. I see now that they just wanted me to write down what happened with them later.

Chapter One

My name is Todd Michael. I'm from Iowa. I used to be a trauma physician. I was a lot of things, *am* a lot of things, but the big thing that really sticks out in my mind after all the dust has settled is that I was a trauma-and-emergency guy. Believe it or not—and I will explain this in due course—I never consciously set out to be such a thing. But it happened and I ended up logging about 25,000 hours doing it.

All in all I would say I was rather mediocre, hardly anything special for an ER doc. I don't want to make myself out to be any great doctor. But I wasn't all that bad either. I got by and, although I made my share of mistakes, I was never sued in all that time. I even was the director of an entire level-three trauma center for about three years. I supervised many other physicians. Really good ones too. Guys I loved. Guys I'd go to bat for. Guys I had to fire sometimes. Guys who burned themselves out sometimes.

I burned myself out over time. As pretty much everyone does at that job, I eventually got to the point where I just couldn't do it anymore. Things—things that I don't really want to talk about anymore—started cropping up that made me ease out of that life.

It starts to work on you after a long time. Maybe some guys can handle it for a lot longer than others. I was about average. You won't see all that many older guys doing that kind of work. And if you do see one, you can almost bet the guy got wiped out by a divorce and is scrambling, desperate to put together some kind of retirement before he reaches the point where something in his emotional or physical makeup finally blows for good. After all, trauma work pays fairly well and you can make a lot of money in a short time if you are willing to really abuse yourself in a major way.

Don't get me wrong, though. Trauma work, emergency work in general, can be incredibly rewarding and really quite a bit of fun in its own way. There are plenty of days when every patient gets better, every diagnosis is immediate and correct, everyone does their job smoothly, and most of the personal interactions are happy and energetic. It's really pretty cool to have all of this mind-boggling technology at your fingertips—the MRIs and the tests and the drugs—and be able to use them to diagnose and fix people who are brought before you at the very worst moments of their lives.

But there are these other days. And they are so stressful that I really don't think you could possibly imagine them in your wildest dreams. Not even with the aid of live or dramatic TV shows. I can't even imagine those days myself now, and I was there. You just can't explain, or show on any screen, how it actually *feels* to be there on that kind of day—watching all kinds of people get ripped apart, families getting ripped apart. You can't really convey what it is like to be mixed up right there with them under the bright operating lights, smartly caffeinated, three or four people all dying simultaneously, really fast, all at the same time, in different bays, and *you're not sure what to do*. You're really not entirely sure. But you're the only doctor in the hospital. So, so late at night after doing this all day long on your typical twenty-four-hour shift. And it's creepy and cold and utterly devoid of anything to smile about, even fleetingly. And you're so, so tired. And having to keep it together perfectly. No matter what. You can't lose it. You can't. There isn't anyone else there that can take over in many instances. And death is all around. All around you.

But I don't want to whine. I really don't. I *promised* myself I wouldn't whine. Or get too terribly dramatic. None of that really matters all that much anyway. What matters, *all* that matters now after it has all passed, are these unusual experiences, powerful spiritual experiences in which I became aware of the presence of God around me and my dying patients. This presence is felt by almost everyone in due course. When your time comes you'll feel it too. And maybe that presence will seem like a messenger or "angel." Maybe you've already felt it.

Actually, they don't call themselves angels. Strictly speaking, there isn't any such thing as an angel. Only God exists—a radiant, loving presence that pervades everything and everyone. The "angels," the "messengers," are just his way of showing himself in such a way that we can actually handle it.

I didn't have a great number of encounters with divine elements in my trauma career. They were relatively few and far between. But I was fortunate enough to record them accurately and in considerable detail when they occurred. This in spite of the fact that I never wanted to talk about these experiences to other people at the time. I really didn't. The experiences you are about to read were very private when they happened and I kept them to myself for a long time. Now I am at a point in my career and my life where I feel comfortable letting people read about them without worrying about what the rest of the doctors might think. Besides, there are so many others like me, so many other doctors that are having their own spiritual experiences that I don't really stick out all that much anymore.

The way I see it, I just don't have any right to withhold the stories in this book any longer. To begin with, they aren't about me. They are about the lives of others, the struggles of others, the deaths of others. More specifically, they are about the important *lessons* these people's lives and deaths illustrate. Real people went through some really bad things and somehow wanted me, *chose* me, to be there with them. I feel that it is therefore my obligation, my duty to make the endings of their precious lives as valuable as possible by telling you what I learned by being there with them.

What makes the lessons and conclusions of this book different and worth reading? The lessons in this book are important because they center largely around the concept that we create our own realities, that our thoughts and intentions actually change the fabric of reality. Although this is an extremely ancient concept and arguably the "great secret" of all the ages, of all the mystical societies of history—and although it has been exhaustively covered in contemporary self-help literature—there are some problems with the notion of self-created reality that have never been adequately addressed. There are some embarrassing paradoxes, some troubling questions inherent in this way of thinking that have troubled me greatly over the years. Questions like these:

• If I create my own reality, why is it so often painful, and so strongly influenced by chance?

- Why is my self-created reality such hard work and so often just plain boring?
- I can think of all sorts of things I would have rather created in my current life—why didn't those things manifest in reality?
- Do I create *all* of my reality or just some of it?
- Do I create reality or does God?
- When am I creating and when is God creating?
- If I try to create a better world for myself by changing my thoughts, aren't I just being selfish and manipulative?
- What are the roles of acceptance, grace, and surrender in a world that responds to conscious intent, in a world that is created and sustained by the psychic and spiritual impetus of individual spirits?
- Is the concept of self-created reality an "un-Christian" notion?
- If I pray for someone else, visualize for someone else, am I then creating part of their reality, or does their life still remain their self-creation?
- If my thoughts create reality, then why do I often have strong and vivid fantasies that never come true, and powerful, insistent fears that never manifest?

In the course of my work, I witnessed a great many deaths, somewhere around five hundred. Over and over I watched as people died in every conceivable way—some as the result of violent automobile or industrial accidents, and some as the result of criminal assault. I attended others who took their own lives through poisoning, hanging, carbon monoxide asphyxiation, slashed wrists, or gunshots to the head. Still others died from acute or chronic illnesses such as heart attacks, strokes, and respiratory failure. Some passed away naturally from "old age" and were transported from nursing homes for me to pronounce dead.

Attending the death of another human being is awe-inspiring, and I regard it as a sacred privilege of the highest order. I am fortunate indeed to have been granted such generous access to an event so incredible. When I witness a soul leaving its body I am deeply humbled and filled with wonder. The power of death is stunning in its intensity. Death changes *everything*, for both the one who dies and for those who are left behind.

During my years of medical practice, first as a family practitioner and then as an emergency and trauma physician, I experienced a major shift in the way I view death and in the way I view my role as a physician. I have always believed the soul survives the death of the body, that something goes on after the heart stops beating, after the lungs stop breathing, after the cellular machinery grinds to a halt. This is not unusual. In spite of what you might believe, the vast majority of physicians are actually quite spiritually aware and believe the soul goes on after the body has fallen away.

Many years ago in the earliest phase of my career I acknowledged and honored the continuity of the soul, but I felt there was little if anything that was required of me after a patient had passed away. Like most doctors, I said a brief prayer and immediately turned my attention to the grieving survivors. There was nothing, I told myself, that I could do now to help my patient. The matter was out of my hands.

But as I saw more and more people die, something within me began to change. I started to wonder: Was it really considerate of me to simply turn away the minute a patient shed his or her physical form? If the soul went on, wasn't it my duty to see what I could do to help? Wasn't it responsible, compassionate, to at least *try*?

And so I began to do just that. After I had pronounced a patient dead, I continued to minister to the being that lay before me. Unbeknownst to those around me—I never discussed this with anyone but my wife—I began to extend myself to the departed soul in a kind of silent communion akin to prayer. I began asking the newly liberated souls of my patients if there was anything I could do to help them.

At first my efforts seemed in vain. I had no sense that anyone was listening, that anyone cared. I even found myself wondering, as we all do from time to time, if there really is a life after death. When I grew discouraged, I often would catch myself thinking that the concept of the soul was just a fanciful construct of the mind, a desperate rationalization, the ego's way of reassuring itself when faced with the stark reality of its final demise.

But I persisted in my attempts because I wasn't sure. If there was any chance at all that the soul was still present after death, I reasoned, then it was my responsibility as a physician and as a human being to make every attempt to ease its suffering during the harrowing transition from this world to the next.

Finally something started to happen, something that changed my life at a very deep level: As I spoke to the departing souls of my patients, I began to sense that they were somehow speaking back to me.

The first few times this happened I was deeply shaken. The logical, sensible part of my mind went into overdrive trying in every way possible to rationalize this phenomenon, to explain it in some reasonable way, in a way that was acceptable to me as a physician and scientist.

But I was not successful. I was receiving very distinct and persistent impressions from the souls that were shedding their earthly forms before me, and they weren't going away. In fact, my new apperceptions grew stronger and more vivid with the passage of time. Before long I found that I was having, in selected instances, substantial conversations with these souls.

And then, as if this weren't enough, something even more astounding began to happen: I began to sense and finally converse with other beings—presences of light and love and wisdom that seemed invariably present during these critical rites of passage. This book is a record of my experiences with these beings, who are manifestations of the one great God who guides us all.

Many hundreds of people have contacted me over the last few years to tell me that they have been experiencing the same thing. Physicians, psychiatrists, and psychologists of every variety, nurses, hospice workers, social workers, and all manner of laypeople have told me that they too have made quiet attempts to speak with God, with his messengers, and even with departed loved ones. Sometimes this has happened in the context of medicine and sometimes in the context of their personal lives. Such "conversations" are quite common and hardly qualify as abnormal or even unusual in this day and age.

How do these conversations occur? I've asked myself the same thing many times. The answer is that I don't really know. Furthermore, I don't really care. I'm not sure it matters. What I do know is that I don't hear any actual voices and I don't see any forms. Neither do I experience any kind of "automatic writing" or "channeling"—it's much more mundane than that. I simply think of questions and, when I do, answers effortlessly flood into my mind. The whole process seems very natural and leaves me with a peaceful feeling. If it didn't I wouldn't have continued the process. I have always looked at the act of typing out the conversations—I'm a very fast typist—as a kind of comforting game I play with myself. I ask myself questions and then *imagine* what a messenger of God would say, or what God himself would say. I've never really known for sure if they are "real."

When one of my friends, Mickey Houlihan, a prominent producer and recording engineer here in Boulder, first read the stories, he told me that whether they were "real" or not was a "stupid question" and a matter of profound indifference. He felt that they *worked,* in the sense that they helped him understand the process of his own life better, and that was what mattered. "Besides," he said, "they can't be just your imagination. This stuff is too smart to be from your mind alone." "Thanks. I think," I answered with a laugh.

I have spoken to many thousands of people in many audiences about these stories in the last few years. I often ask audience members three questions. First, I ask how many members of the audience have survived the death of a loved one. Nearly everyone raises their hand. Next, I ask how many people have said something, however simple, to someone who has just passed away. This could be something as basic as "I wish I would have told you I loved you more often." Again, nearly everyone raises their hand. Finally, I ask how many people have felt at some point as though something—an impression, a message, an emotion—was being returned to them in some way. The hands go up more slowly this time. But what continually amazes me is how many of the hands still go up.

I tell people that the only difference between what they have done and what I have done is a matter of degree. Having attended more than five hundred deaths during the course of my career, I have had many chances to experience and practice this type of communication process.

One of the most important things you should know is that as I have written this book, I have grown increasingly certain that it doesn't take any special skill or talent to communicate at a higher spiritual level. If there is but a single message this book conveys, I hope it is this: *God and his messengers are freely accessible to every human being at every moment, without exception.*

Chapter Two

Amy was a beautiful little girl and well loved. At the age of eight, she suffered an untimely and violent death. We knew something very bad had happened as soon as the first call came in over the scanner. The EMTs told us they were at eleven thousand feet on the big mountain at the ski resort nearby, frantically trying to save a girl who had slammed into a tree at high velocity. She was in full cardiac arrest. Bystanders started CPR immediately after the accident and the crew was now doing everything they could to keep her alive.

I talked to them on the radio as they brought her in, halfheartedly giving them medication orders. The situation seemed hopeless. Her heart had stopped beating nearly an hour before. Survival after this amount of time was rare. It seemed that my only job would be to pronounce her dead. Then the unexpected happened. By some miracle the ambulance crew established a rudimentary heartbeat three blocks away from the hospital.

That changed everything.

I called everybody in stat. Fifteen professionals were waiting when Amy came through the door: surgery, anesthesia, respiratory, lab, radiology, and an anxious throng of nurses from the ICU. A frenzy of coordinated activity ensued.

Amy's heart was terribly weak and very slow. I placed a pacemaker and injected the usual drugs. For a few minutes it looked like we might bring her around. But I couldn't get a consistent rhythm going and she continued to deteriorate. A few minutes later, two of the other docs wanted to call it quits, but I shook my head. There was still a very small chance. This was somebody's beloved daughter and we had to try everything again and again and again. The parents were going to look into our eyes and ask. We had to be able to tell them we had done everything humanly possible. Who would demand less for their child?

Fifteen minutes later, drenched in sweat, I just nodded and everybody stopped. No one spoke. I went into the chapel where the parents were kneeling in urgent prayer. They turned and looked into my eyes. I didn't say it, I couldn't somehow, but they immediately saw it in my face. The mother collapsed into our arms. The anguish I witnessed during the next half hour was beyond description.

Finally, I led the parents back to the ER, where they pressed their tearstained faces against their daughter's cold cheeks and told her again and again how much they loved her. They were good people, deep people. Even in their agony they found the strength to think of others: They courageously offered to donate their child's organs. I was humbled, even shamed by the depth of their selflessness, their dignity in the face of this horror.

But my job wasn't over. There was still the girl. I knew she was nearby. I could feel her. She was confused and disoriented. I went back into the call room, which was only twenty feet from where she lay in her mother's arms, and it began.

Can I help you? Are you okay?

[Silence.]

Is anyone there?

Mommy? I want my mommy. [Silence.] *Why can't Mommy hear me?*

[Pause.] She just can't hear you right now.

Daddy? Are you my daddy?

No. I'm your doctor. My name is Michael. I want to try to help you. You've had a very bad accident.

[As if in a dream.] *What is that sound? What is that ringing, all that buzzing? Why am I up here? Why can't I come down? I can't hold still. Why is everything moving like that?* [Crying.] *I feel funny. Mommy?*

You are in your spirit now. You have to relax. You *have* to. Just pretend you're lying back. Don't fight this, just relax. I promise you, you are going to be okay.

Why is it so bright? Am I hurt? I don't feel hurt. I feel so good. Why is Mommy crying? Can't you make her stop crying? Mommy? Why does she look like that?

She just can't hear you right now. She's praying. She's just sad because your spirit came out of your body. I'll help her. There are a lot of people here to help her. She says she loves you very much.

[Pause. And then, speaks as if to another.] *Who are you? It's so bright. What is that? What is that shiny thing?*

[New voice.] *I am your messenger mother.*

Are you my mommy? [Pause.] *Are you my grandma?*

I am your messenger mother.

[Pause.] *I know you. Don't I? Why can't I...did I forget you?* [Pause.] *I'm so glad to see you.*

Where have you been? I missed you so much. You're so pretty.

So are you.

Why are we up here? What is Mommy looking at? Is that me? It looks like me.

No. You are right here with me.

What is that sound? Everything is buzzing. [Pause.] *Can I go home? I want to go home. Can Mommy come? Daddy?*

I'll take you home. Mommy and Daddy will come a little later. Do you want to play?

Then there was silence. The call room suddenly seemed so empty. I thought I would try something.

Is there anybody there? Who are you? Can you hear me?

Yes. We are with you, and we can hear you.

Is she okay? Is there anything more I can do for her? For you?

She is being cared for. All is well. Her passing has been eased.

Who are you?

You know who we are. I am the one of us who speaks.

Is there just one of you or several?

We are many and yet only one.

You seem so…familiar. Do I know you?

[Soft laughter.] *Yes. More than the others, I have a special interest in you for various reasons. Just keep in mind that it isn't quite that simple. There is no distinct "me." I shift and change, merging, flowing in and out of the others. A group of us tend to congregate with one another. One or more of us may help you or speak with you on any given occasion.*

What are the "various reasons" you speak of?

[Pause.] *Let's just say you know me. You know me very well indeed. If you had any idea….We have been together for a long, long time.*

What do you mean? Before I was born?

Yes. We have been together in many ways, in many roles with each other. In fact, you were once my messenger and, in due course, you will be my messenger again.

Were we alive together here on Earth before?

I didn't say that exactly. It's not quite that simple. All in good time. Suffice it to say, for now, that we have known each other a long, long time, and I will be with you for the rest of your life. I will never leave you.

Why are you here today, with the little girl that died?

I am not at a place and I am not with her. I am with you.

But why can I hear you just now?

You don't always listen in this way.

So you are not the one here to help this girl? There are others?

I told you we are many, and yet we are only one.

You say I know you. [*Pause.*] I feel bad that I have forgotten you. You seem to know me so well, but I can't quite remember you even though you seem so terribly familiar in a way.

Don't feel bad. We discussed this before you went down. We both knew that it would be this way, that the veil would be drawn and that you would for-get for a time. That was part of the deal. Nobody there remembers. But you will. All of you will remember in time. And all of you will return.

Does everybody have a messenger like you?

Everybody that wants a messenger has a messenger, but they aren't all like me. Having a messenger is the default mode, so to speak. Unless you specify oth-erwise, before or after you are born, you are automatically accompanied by one or more messengers. But very few souls specifically ask to be without a messenger. That wouldn't make any sense.

[*Silence.*] This is crazy. Am I imagining you?

Of course. [Laughing.] All communication with Spirit takes place through the imagination. The imagination, the part of the mind that can synthesize images, is one of the highest faculties of the mind. Don't knock it. It is the end product of several billion years of painstaking evolution. Second only to love, the ability to imagine makes human beings sons and daughters of the great Creator. All creation, all great accomplishment, and all communication with the Spirit begins within the imagination.

Your real question lies within your question. You are really asking, "Do we exist as real beings independent of your mind?" The answer is yes. We exist independently of you and are in many ways far more "real" than you.

Don't misunderstand. Although the faculty of imagination enables you to hear us, we are not "imaginary" as such. We are not mere figments of your imagination, mere fantasy. The words that are forming in your mind are real words from real beings.

Why have you chosen to speak with me?

It is you who have chosen to speak with us.

What I mean is, why will you speak with me and not the others? Of all people, why can I hear you? This doesn't make any sense at all to me. I'm an idiot!

[Laughter.] We're all idiots. Your question contains a faulty assumption—that we include and exclude other people in our communications. That is not the case. We speak to everyone all the time. We are channels of the Spirit, and Spirit communicates freely from every point of consciousness to every other point of consciousness at every moment.

Then why can I "hear" your words while others can't?

Again, your question contains an unspoken assumption—that others cannot, in fact, hear us. All beings can hear all of the words and music of Spirit all the time. It's a matter of awareness. Most of you are simply not paying attention. You are focused solely on the constant stimuli you surround yourselves with and on your incessant internal dialogue. You are lost in confusion and self-doubt and have lost the ability to know that what you are hearing is Spirit. Animals, infants, the very elderly, and certain others hear us clearly and constantly. Without the burden of self-doubt, they are free to hear us effortlessly.

Many adults, however, are hearing us more clearly now. Many more than you realize. Like you, they cannot integrate this into their daily lives and responsibilities and therefore remain conflicted and secretive about it.

[Pause.] I'm still having a problem with this. Let me rephrase the question. Why am I conscious of you while others are not?

Certain experiences in your life have caused your ego and internal dialogue to erode sufficiently so that you can distinguish our voices from time to time. Your

years of meditation have been helpful. Certain misfortunes that you have expe-
rienced, certain periods of inner suffering have also helped. Nothing is wasted.
Nothing is random. Every misfortune, every tragedy, every "sickness" is a step
toward the light.

In addition, we have watched you and know that you, like most other physi-
cians, are often involved with souls passing from your dimension to our own.
You have a rudimentary understanding and appreciation of the beyond that is
favorable and facilitates communication. I, in particular, have a stong interest in
facilitating your understanding—we'll talk more about this in time.

But most important, you believe that we are present and have made a simple
effort to communicate. This, more than anything, has helped you perceive us.
Anyone who believes we are present can, with a little practice and a little faith,
speak with us easily.

I feel very much at ease speaking with you but very uneasy
revealing this to others. Even my friends would likely shun me if
they knew I was doing this.

All of your friends and all the members of your family, virtually without
exception, are very wise beings within, very experienced. They know far more
than you realize, far more than they themselves realize. It is true they will experi-
ence doubts and judgments regarding this, but in time they will understand. In
fact, all of them are themselves on the brink of similar states of communication.
They have their own internal struggles with acceptance. Let them think what
they will. They mean no harm. [Pause.] You have many questions.

Well, the first thing I suppose I would like to know is, what are
you? What are messengers exactly?

We are like the leaves of a tree. There are myriad leaves on a tree, but they are
all part of a larger organism. A great diamond has many individual facets but
they are all surfaces of a single jewel.

So it is with God. This Being of Beings has many individual beings or "cells"
within its body, and each is an integral part of a single infinite organism.

There is only one jewel, one being, one light, one Mind. The great religions of your world have made this clear for thousands of years. There is nothing separate from this being. Every subatomic particle, every molecule, every rock, every star, every animal, every plant, every human being, and every messenger is a perfectly integrated component of the great chain of being that is Love's body.

When learning about the messengers of Spirit, always keep this foremost in mind: When you are dealing with a messenger, you are dealing with God. Don't get confused about this. It's very straightforward.

Are you saying that when I am talking to you, I am talking to God? Surely you don't mean to suggest that I am talking to God right now.

Of course. Everyone is talking to God right now. When you talk to me you are talking to God. When you talk to a child you are talking to God. When you talk to the most aggravating person you know, you are talking to God. If you speak to a rock you are talking to God and, for that matter, when you are talking to yourself you are talking to God.

Is that what I'm doing right now, talking to myself?

God, your "self," your "messenger," it's all the same. You just have so many different names for things, so many words, that you confuse yourself. You should be more like an infant. An infant calls everything "da" and thus suffers no confusion. That's part of the reason babies can perceive us so clearly.

This is a little much for me right now. I suppose I'll stick with thinking of you simply as a messenger for the time being.

[Laughter.] *That's perfectly fine. Easy does it.*

[*Pause.*] Forgive me, but I still need clarification about something: You said that messengers are simply fragments, rays, of the one great light. It is difficult for me to understand why Spirit doesn't simply remain as one single undivided entity. Why has the Spirit divided itself into many small pieces of life and light?

You still don't get it. The Spirit is not divided. It is always as one. Messengers, like you, are simply a part of that oneness. Perhaps the best way to understand why we exist as apparent fragments of the one light is to understand our purpose. Actually, we serve several important functions. Most important, we increase Spirit's accessibility.

In what way?

You have to understand that the concerted energy and intelligence of the great Being of Beings is vast beyond comprehension. The full presence of this source of infinite light is too awesome, too potent, too overwhelming for human beings to accommodate. If Spirit were to reveal its full light to you, it would be like connecting a high tension line to a tiny lightbulb. The results would be devastating.

The energy of the Spirit flows like electricity?

There are similarities. When electrical power is delivered to your home it has to be "stepped down" so that it is safe. As it travels from the power station to your home it passes through a series of transformers that channel decreasing amounts of power into smaller and smaller wires or channels. Thus energy is delivered in a way that is safe and manageable. The wiring and appliances in your home were never designed to handle large amounts of power.

Messengers are Spirit's way of revealing itself, of channeling itself in a way that can be safely tolerated by human beings. Think of us as the precision instruments Spirit uses to render personal, individualized care.

Would it also be correct to say that messengers are a kind of buffer system designed to protect humans from the full force of the light?

Yes. But this step-down system has other advantages. This arrangement also increases Spirit's flexibility and dexterity.

How?

It is said that human beings are made in the image of God. Look at your arm. At the end it tapers to a series of individual fingers, each with an intricate system of delicate muscles. Without them your arm would be powerful but incapable of finely controlled motion. Fingers enable a human being to play a piano sonata, perform a delicate and lifesaving surgical procedure, or weave a beautiful and complex tapestry.

Messengers are God's fingers. Like the fingers on your hand, we operate in a perfectly coordinated fashion to execute the fine details of the great design. Like the fine tools of a master jeweler, we enable the infinite power of Spirit to work with the delicate chains of cause and effect that characterize the lives of individual beings.

We are also a kind of face or "storefront" that allows the infinite power and intelligence of Spirit to assume a personal, user-friendly form. It is easier for some creatures to develop a personal relationship with Spirit with this system. [Laughter.] Most people in your world would prefer the form of a small, pleasantly featured man or woman to that of a trillion suns. There's only so much you can handle.

How do messengers come into being? Are you created from nothingness or are you formed from something that already exists?

As I told you, we are channels of Spirit. We are not created from nothingness—no creature is ever created anew from a void. All beings are facets of the great Being of Beings, which continually transforms and recycles itself.

Practically speaking, most messengers are souls that are either waiting to take birth or have already been on Earth and since passed on. Some, but not all, messengers have a natural interest in people on your plane. Some may even take a particular interest in human beings who have been related to them in some way.

Are there any bad or "evil" messengers?

Of course not. Although there are myths about "dark messengers" and "evil messengers," these are backward and ignorant notions—remnants of medieval times when organized religion, with a fear-based philosophy, was used as a tool to control the masses.

God is everything, and God is pure love. Period. All of his creatures, all of his messengers are extensions of this love. Everything else that apparently exists is but ego and illusion. If you want to understand the Bible and other similar holy books, all you have to do is substitute the word "ego" whenever you read "evil" or "devil."

That sounds like A Course in Miracles.

It sounds like a lot of sources. All truth comes from the same place.

Let me make sure I understand you clearly. Are you saying there is no form of organized conspiracy of evil anywhere in the universe? There is no devil?

You know better than that.

I just need to hear you say it.

The term "organized evil" is an impossible contradiction—what you would call an oxymoron. The term "organized evil" is like the term "organized chaos" or "ordered disorder"—it doesn't make any sense.

Mathematicians say there actually is order within chaos.

[Laughter.] That is true—up to a point. Actually, a better way of saying it is that there is no chaos, only apparent chaos from certain limited points of observation.

God is the great organizing principle in the universe, the force that creates order. It is this order that makes life, love, knowledge, and beauty possible when they would otherwise be impossible. No sequence of random events in a purely random universe could ever explain the origin of life and the evolution of God-conscious beings that has occurred on Earth—however appealing that theory may be to some individuals.

There is a certain element of entropy that is intentionally built into the system to keep it from becoming stagnant. This force is a part of God. Without a force to keep some things from falling apart, everything would reach a state of perfect, crystalline perfection. This would be a frozen, motionless, lifeless state of affairs in which nothing new could be created.

This all sounds very tidy but no matter how you cut it, there are still some very bad people out there doing very bad things.

Yes, there are confused people, malignant rulers, even malignant empires that have come upon the Earth. As you will come to understand, free will isn't really free. It comes with a price. In the big picture such phenomena are simply part of the entropy that keeps things from becoming stagnant. But these kinds of negative processes are in no way organized by some great conspiracy. No matter how well organized they might appear up close, from a larger perspective they are forces of entropy and subject to its tendencies. They are constantly falling apart. This is why they cannot sustain themselves and invariably self-destruct over time. Witness the fact that all the great evils have extinguished themselves over time while all the great religions are still alive and growing.

Does entropy exist in your world?

Here, things are different. Certainly, there are confused and egotistical people on Earth. But there are no evil spirits or evil messengers in our world. Any psychic or other "expert" who claims differently is gravely mistaken. Any malicious spirit or entity that is "perceived" is in fact created by the observer's troubled subconscious. The terms "evil spirit" or "dark messenger" are also oxymorons. They make no more sense than the terms "hateful love" or "dark light."

I'll make this very clear for you: There are no goblins, demons, ghosts, ghouls, monsters, trolls, gnomes, vampires, werewolves, or bogeymen. Further, sorcery, black magic, Voodoo, witchcraft, and Satanism are all pure delusion—they have absolutely no power to summon any "organized" supernatural forces.

That's all in people's heads. Without exception, these notions are but the fantasies of disturbed people, people in a great deal of pain, people who for one reason or another cannot see their own pure love within. If you want to walk with the messengers, cast off these ridiculous concepts and turn your attention fully toward the light.

Are you sure that little girl is going to be all right?

Yes, she is doing beautifully. She is in very good hands.

Is there anything more I can do to help her or her family?

Nothing in the conventional sense, no. You have done all that can be done as a physician. But you can pray for her family. Send them light and love and we will make sure the energy you send arrives to help them.

Chapter Three

Although he had long since lost his mind, Dr. C. was still an amazing client. In his lifetime he had seen over a quarter million patients. Now, ravaged by Alzheimer's and a series of devastating strokes, he lay in a nursing home unable to feed himself or recognize his own wife.

I didn't care. He was still a healer. It was my job to render him the finest care I was capable of providing. Besides, when I looked at him, I saw myself lying there helpless. I knew that I could easily end up this way someday too. And so I talked to him and brought him things from time to time—he liked sweets—and I also took good care of his wife, who was a patient and a friend.

That beautiful spring day, I wanted to go directly home to work in the garden after a long day at work. But as I drove home, I suddenly had an inexplicable urge to see him.

I rang the bell at the Alzheimer's unit and the electronic lock flipped open. Suddenly, as I passed through the heavy door, a siren went off and the overhead blared, "Code Blue in room 732." It was the old doctor.

As I ran toward his room I suddenly collided with two other

anxious individuals. One was his minister, the other his wife. By some miracle all three of us had converged at his room simultaneously as he arrested. We entered his room and waved the nurses and the approaching crash cart away just in the nick of time.

His wife had begged me to protect him from any extraordinary efforts when his time came. We just stood around his bed and held his withered hands as the color slowly drained from his distinguished and kindly face.

His wife cried briefly but no one was really sad. Far from it. We had prayed for years that he would be released quickly, for he had suffered mightily in his final years. The minister said a prayer, I lingered with his wife, who seemed deeply relieved, and finally went out to my car.

As I drove away I turned the radio on. Eric Clapton's plaintive voice sang to his child who had died tragically at an early age.

Would you know my name, if I saw you in heaven?
Would it be the same, if I saw you in heaven.
Beyond the door, there's peace for sure.

Of all the songs to come on at just that time. It was an eerie but very beautiful moment. Goose bumps stood up all over my body. I thought I felt Doc there in the car with me for a few minutes. But I shook it off, telling myself it was just my imagination. But the sensation persisted. As I arrived home, I began to speak with him silently.

Are you okay?
Of course.
How is it there?

Beautiful, of course!

Do you mind if I ask you something personal?

[Laughing.] *You are my doctor. That's your job, isn't it?*

Well, something has been bothering me for a long time. I watched you become increasingly demented for the last few years and I found this quite disturbing.

Flattery will get you nowhere!

You know, they all said you were quite a jokester in your younger years, before I came on the scene. I guess you haven't changed. But seriously, the same thing happened to my grandmother. She was a near vegetable for the last ten years of her life. She was a very beautiful, spiritual person all her life but at the end she was angry, combative, and even profane. I always thought that didn't make any sense—for her to lose her spiritual beauty and peace. It seemed completely unfair.

She never lost anything. She just moved like I did: Nice and easy.

What do you mean?

It's like this: On Earth there are two ways to move from one house to another: All at once, or gradually in stages. Some people wait until the last minute and have the movers come in and do everything in one day. Others pack very methodically for months in advance and take a load or two over to the new house every few days.

It's a matter of preference. Your grandmother and I moved very slowly and carefully. The boxes that contained our wisdom and our spiritual knowledge were moved to the other side many years before we finally pulled out of our bodies. That's why we appeared to lose our minds from your side. It was a lot easier that way for me. I just couldn't face the suddenness of the other way. Too harsh. Too disorganized. Besides, what's the hurry? Incidentally, this works the other way too. Most people aren't exactly born all at once either.

What do you mean by that?

I mean that when your body takes form on the earthly plane, your angelic consciousness usually doesn't complete the transition in one fell swoop. You remain part angel, as it were, during your infancy and childhood.

Is that why children look like messengers? I know children who I would swear are part messenger.

Actually, they are messengers much of the time. Many small children still have one foot in this world. Many souls prefer to ease gradually into the relatively harsh conditions of the physical plane.

Would you mind if I asked you a few other things?

[Laughter.] Go ahead.

Are you a messenger now?

[More laughter.] Of course.

What do you—what do messengers actually look like?

Well, you are familiar with the traditional images of a messenger—the winged figure surrounded by light, the stranger with a beautiful face who appears mysteriously to resolve a crisis, then vanishes without a trace—these are the images made popular in books and movies.

We can indeed appear in such ways and it makes quite an impression when we do. But it is critical to understand that we manifest in this way very rarely. When we are present and working among you, we become visible or audible less than one time in a million.

We have a kind of "prime directive" that we strive to follow at all times: We are strictly prohibited from making ourselves audible or visible except in very special circumstances and then only after receiving special permission.

Why is this? Why don't you show yourselves to us more often? This doesn't make any sense at all. Wouldn't it help increase our faith and our understanding of the light if we could just see you and talk with you normally?

Absolutely not. To understand why we stay transparent, you have to remember why you are there on Earth in the first place. Your foremost goal as human beings is to learn to transcend your senses. Your job is to develop your souls—to strengthen your abilities to think and act and communicate at the level of Spirit. By remaining above your plane, we consistently encourage you to progress in consciousness toward our level.

Effective teachers always act this way, always keeping the bar high for their students. Consider how a good foreign language teacher on Earth encourages her students to become more proficient. The teacher always speaks in the language to be learned, rarely, if ever, lapsing into the pupil's native tongue. This strengthens the student's ability to communicate effectively in the new language immeasurably.

If we constantly made ourselves visible, how would this serve the greater plan? It would only reinforce your tendency to look at things through worldly eyes. In the short run it might give you a powerful spiritual boost, but in the long run it would actually weaken you and stunt your spiritual growth.

This is why we become visible very, very sparingly—just enough to let a person know but once or twice that we exist. Then we go back to the level of Spirit knowing that you will learn to speak the language of Spirit if we are patient and diligent in our instruction. Look at yourself: It worked for you.

Here in the spirit realm it is considered very clumsy and unprofessional to become noticeable while performing one's duties. We take great pride in remaining subtle and transparent while doing our job.

Are you actually invisible while you are doing your job, or are you just so unobtrusive that we don't notice you?

Actually, you are seeing us all the time but you are seldom aware that you are observing us. Most of you wouldn't recognize one of us if we bit you on the nose. For example, we could manifest as a mosquito buzzing around your head at just the right moment. As you pause to swat this apparently annoying insect, the chain of events that follows—your personal web of cause and effect—is altered slightly but very precisely. An hour or a day later a traffic accident is narrowly averted, a "chance" encounter with an important person takes place, or you arrive at home just in time to receive a crucial phone call.

Do you have any limitations as to how you can manifest, or can you appear in any way you wish?

We have few, if any, limitations in how we may appear. We may be animate or inanimate, beautiful or repulsive, impressive or mundane. We may be astronomically large or microscopic. We could manifest as a rainbow, a scrap of trash, a sequence in a dream, a rainstorm, a digital impulse on the Internet, a blown fuse, or gust of wind. The image we project could last a nanosecond or a billion years.

We could manifest as a car driving too slowly in front of you, making you "late" for an appointment. We could be an animal crossing your path, a retarded person staring at you in a checkout line, a leaf falling into a pond that grabs your attention at just the right moment, a ragged homeless person asking you for money, or a small child smiling at you on the bus. I'm telling you, you're seeing us all the time.

Then you are saying that anything and everything could be a messenger?

Yes. For this reason, it is wise to treat everyone as if they were a messenger, a direct extension of God. Be careful. Any stranger, any living creature you encounter may actually be a messenger. Don't make a fool of yourself by being rude or aloof to a messenger of the divine.

When you are not manifesting here as you have described, do you have a form of some kind? What are you made of exactly?

[Pause.] To understand our true nature, think for a minute about an amoeba. An amoeba is a bit of living protoplasm enclosed by a single continuous cell wall. This protoplasm can form projections called pseudopods. From certain limited viewpoints, these projections might appear to have a life of their own. But they do not. They remain attached to the larger organism at all times and derive their energy from it.

This is how we are. We are projections of the Great Spirit, the Great Light. Although we appear in some ways to be independent, self-contained creatures, we are not. For that matter, neither are you.

So you are made of light?

Yes and no. We are even finer and more etheric than light itself. We are very nearly pure consciousness. But for all practical purposes you may think of us as beings of light.

I still don't quite understand. Do you have a distinct "body" that is made of light?

Not exactly. As I said, we are best described as fluid beings. We move and change ourselves constantly. We shift and flow, much like a candle flame or a rivulet of water flowing over a surface. This is one of the main differences between us and human beings who are caught in a relatively stable form.

You also flow and change, although you are not generally conscious of this. Nearly all of the molecules in your body are replaced by new molecules every year. Your bodies are like sandbars in a river. The river is constantly washing away grains of sand on one side while new grains are simultaneously added to the other side. The sandbar appears to remain stationary and stable in the current when, in reality, it is constantly flowing.

The difference between us and you is a matter of degree. We are both fluid and changing, but messengers flow and change much more freely and much more quickly than humans. Whereas you may take months or years to change your form, we can shift and change from instant to instant with the speed of thought. We have escaped the illusion of solidity so completely that we flow perfectly and with no effort.

There are so many things I would like to ask you. I don't know where to begin.

Take your time. I'm not going anywhere. [Laughter.]

I am very uneasy asking you about specific information, about specific people and events. Should I be asking you these kinds of questions?

You can ask anything you want. But one of the things I've always liked about you is that you aren't much interested in minutiae. You seem to have a natural preoccupation with the bigger questions. Like I say, you can ask anything you want. I may even answer some specific kinds of questions. But be careful. You should think very carefully before you ask. Do you really want to know specifics about the future?

No. Not really. If something good is going to happen, it's going to happen and that will be great. If I know in advance, I'll just be frustrated with what I have now and grow impatient. On the other hand, if something bad is going to happen to me, I'll worry and fret and dread the pain involved, and my life will be hell. Either way, I'd much rather be surprised.

Oh, be honest. You would love to know which companies are going to do well in the stock market, now, wouldn't you? [Laughter.] No, the answer you have given is the best one by and large. But there is a problem with your statement. Look at what you have said. Do you see the fatalism in your words? Aren't you implying that you have no control when you talk about things happening "to you"?

Well, maybe I didn't say that in the best way. [*Pause.*] Actually, I believe that we create our own realities and that we can decide to some degree what will happen to us. We aren't just helpless victims waiting for external random forces to do as they will.

That is correct. Once you know this you can begin to see why it doesn't make any sense to ask us what is going to happen "to you." If we were to tell you, then we would be taking away your ability to decide for yourself, to create your own world, your own dreams. Can you see how that would be horribly unethical?

Yes. That seems to make sense. [*Silence.*] Let me ask you something else: Do messengers have specific names? How should I refer to you?

[*Hearty laughter.*] *You can refer to us in any way you want. We don't care about such things. Names do not exist here. They are completely irrelevant on this plane. To name us wouldn't make any more sense than to name a flowing, ephemeral pseudopod on an amoeba.*

Chapter Four

For years I had a standing order for all the receptionists: If an Amish person comes through the doors, you are to summon me immediately, even if there appears to be no obvious emergency. The Amish only consult a doctor when they are gravely ill.

Rebecca was a beautiful, angelic Amish mother in her mid-thirties. When I first saw her, she displayed no obvious signs of illness. She was standing neatly dressed in the waiting room, tending quietly to her eight children. Appearances can be deceiving.

In the privacy of the examination room she told me she had fallen two stories through a plate glass window. She said she had a "little cut" on her chest that she had been treating at home with herbs and poultices and prayer. As it turned out, a long shard of glass had penetrated her thorax and her right lung was completely collapsed. Two weeks had elapsed since the accident. Until now, she had continued to work as usual at home.

Things got worse. A lot worse. When I worked her up, I discovered she also had breast cancer, a very advanced case. A bone scan showed that tumors had already metastasized throughout her body.

All the clan's elders were called in. They came from as far as

Vermont. About a week later, twelve of them met with me in the chapel of the hospital, their long white beards and all-black clothes creating quite a sensation. As they listened intently to my words, I told them I held a deep respect for their healing ways, for their herbs, their vitamins, and most of all for their prayers. But I told them in no uncertain terms that they would have to add additional treatment modalities to these. Modern medical techniques would be required if Rebecca's life was to be saved.

They considered my advice with great care for two days. Ultimately, however, they declined. Rebecca was not to have surgery, chemotherapy, or medication of any kind.

Unable to afford the fare for a companion, she set off alone on a train with no air-conditioning in mid-August for an alternative clinic in southern Mexico to receive shark cartilage therapy.

By this time both of her lungs were collapsing periodically. Along with her simple black suitcase, she carried two special water seal devices connected to chest tubes designed to keep each lung inflated. When she returned three weeks later she had lost another thirty pounds. Never complaining, she died quietly in the hospital four days later. Thankfully, she accepted pain medication at the end.

We did everything we could to help her family. We wrote off thousands of dollars in medical care and did our best to ease the suffering of her loved ones. Several messengers were present at the end. After she was ushered to the other side, I began asking them questions.

Do you mind if I ask you a few things?

Of course not. Have we ever given you the impression that we feel this is a problem?

No. You have always been very helpful. Is she going to be all right?

Yes, she is so much better now. You needn't worry about her or her family. We will take care of them.

But the children, eight of them—what will they do? They have no mother. No messenger can possibly take her place.

Of course not. Their suffering is beyond description. But there is a reason. There is always a reason.

[Angrily.] What reason? What can possibly justify such a catastrophic event? For the love of God, there are eight innocent children involved.

Suffice it to say, all of them agreed on this course of action. They all decided this path would help them progress in spirit more efficiently than any other path. If you could see ahead—and behind—from our vantage point, you would immediately understand. They have been incredibly wise and incredibly courageous in their choice. They will be together again in time, and their bonds of love will be immeasurably strengthened. Please be at peace with this. Leave them to us. Turn your attention to the job at hand. Ask the things you want to know.

[Silence.] One of the things I have really wanted to ask is, what are messengers attracted to? How can we encourage your presence among us, among those we want to help?

It is often said that opposites attract, and in many instances this is true. The positive pole of a magnet attracts the negative pole of another magnet. Male and female are attracted to one another. Quiet people often like to be around people who talk a lot and vice versa.

But in many other cases like attracts like. Throughout the universe, massive astronomical bodies are attracted to other bodies with great mass. The attractive force responsible for this is known as gravity, the force that holds your solar system and your galaxy together and your bodies to the Earth.

Like attracts like on many other levels. Young people are attracted to other young people and seniors to other seniors. Positive, charitable, peaceful people much prefer the company of others with similar attitudes.

The principle of like attracting like exerts its influence very strongly in the spirit realm: Messengers are clearly attracted to each other, as well as to human beings who share their way of looking at things. For this reason, anyone seeking to deepen their relationship with us should know something about our mind-set and strive to emulate it.

What are the characteristics of the messenger mind-set?

Our general outlook is characterized by perfect positivity, optimism, and love. We harbor no negativity of any kind. Even the most subtle forms of discouragement, fear, judgment, and malice are unknown to us. We are invariably cheerful, easygoing, and perfectly accepting of others.

But above all, our mind-set is characterized by an incredibly deep sense of appreciation. We savor all we behold in creation and feel a gratitude so deep and so constant that it defies description.

[Silence.] What are messengers like to be around? Are some of you earnest and serious, or are you all fun-loving and full of laughter?

Some messengers are earnest and sober. Some of us are extremely concerned about the suffering we know you feel, and we take our work very seriously. But most of us are quite jubilant and gleeful. The words jolly, rapturous, silly, and mirthful describe the typical messenger. But all of us, including those of us who are somewhat solemn, are happy and deeply contented.

I've noticed you all seem to laugh and joke around quite a bit.

[Laughing.] This is true. We love humor and laugh often and loudly. In fact, you can't imagine how hard and how often we laugh. Even the most whimsical of your comedians could not compete with us. In fact, they derive their inspiration directly from us in many cases. So many of your classical impressions of messengers cast us as somber, businesslike creatures, but these are largely incorrect. Even the Christ and the Source itself are brimming with light and laughter.

How, exactly, are we to use this information?

Realize that when you are in a similar state of mind—positive, accepting, grateful, and joyful—you attract our company automatically by the law of like attracting like. If you are interested in messengers and seek to improve your relationship with us, you would be well advised to abandon any form of negativity.

Watch yourself. Know yourself. Root out every form of doubt, irritation, and anxiety. Be thorough and ruthless in your housecleaning, paying special attention to subtle forms of judgment and pessimism. Every day, without exception, maintain your vigilance.

Constantly strive to lighten your state of mind. A suitable mantra for one seeking the company of messengers is the simple phrase "lighten up." Repeat these words over and over and over, applying them to every difficult situation you encounter throughout your day.

Above all, cultivate a deep and abiding sense of gratitude. Work at this diligently. Dwell in the present and look for the positive in each and every moment. Be proactive in this area. Don't wait for things to appreciate, find things to appreciate. Make time to have fun. Laugh easily and often. Then, we will naturally gravitate toward you and gladly help make your life easier.

Are there any things we should make an effort to avoid?

There are certain things you should avoid like the plague. Strenuously avoid the company of those who complain and condemn. Actively seek the company of those who love life, those who look upon their fellow men and women with love and compassion. Shift your entire mind-set to one of constant optimism and joy.

Break away from any social, political, or religious group that harbors the slightest undertone of judgment or superiority.

Be wary of the books and periodicals you read, the television shows and movies you watch, and the radio programs and music you listen to. These can carry unsettling subliminal messages.

Now you've got me a little worried about something. We are only human. We can't always be positive—that's just not realistic. Are you saying that if we have real problems and react with grief or sadness or frustration that you will be automatically driven away? That doesn't seem fair somehow.

It is true that like attracts like and that it is advisable to maintain a positive state of mind in order to cultivate a healthy relationship with us. But we know that you are human and occasionally vulnerable to various forms of negativity even when you are trying your hardest. This is only natural.

Does this mean that if you are having a difficult time we will abandon you? Of course not. We will never abandon you. There is nothing you can say, nothing you can do to make us stop loving you. It's just that when you are in a positive state you make our job easier and encourage deeper and more frequent contact.

I'm not quite clear about this.

[Laughter.] To understand how this works, imagine for a moment that you are a proud and devoted grandparent. Imagine that you have been left to baby-sit a room full of your grandchildren while the parents go out shopping. At first, all of your beloved grandchildren play quietly and your job is easy. Soon, however, it becomes apparent that one of the children has a problem. Nothing seems to please this child. He begins to whine about everything and begins to quarrel with you and the other children.

Being a perfect grandparent, you take all of this in stride. You love this grandbaby beyond measure. There is absolutely nothing any of your grandchildren could ever say or do to make you stop loving them. What's more, it is utterly unthinkable that you would ever stop watching and protecting them—especially for something as minor as being in a bad mood.

But you are experienced and wise. You know that the worst thing you can do with a whiny child is to give him more attention. More attention reinforces the undesirable behavior. It says to the child, "Whining and complaining is a successful and productive strategy. When you whine, you will get exactly what you want—more of my attention."

You know that the best course of action is to continue watching the child, making sure he doesn't hurt himself while quietly busying yourself with another grandchild who is having fun with a constructive project on the other side of the room. You wait until the child settles down and begins to play quietly. You then reward this behavior by giving him your time and attention.

This is how we see you when you are indulging in unnecessary negativity. Don't act like a spoiled brat over every trivial problem, which is what most of you do when you don't get your way.

Sure, there will be times when you have real problems and times when you will experience real fear about real dangers. Without a doubt, we will be right there to help you when any true difficulty arises. Just be careful. Before you start complaining and throwing a fit, make sure your grievances are genuine and significant.

What should we do if we make a mistake and fall into a negative, ungrateful state of mind?

First of all, don't feel guilty. Never hang on to shame or remorse when dealing with us. If you stray from the path in some way, don't mope around wearing the hair shirt. That just compounds the problem. Snap out of it. Forgive yourself and move on. We have no capacity for judgment or blame. Acting as if we do insults our forgiving and accepting nature.

What else can we do to encourage your presence?

Give something back. If you want to have a healthy, sustainable relationship with a messenger, you cannot expect to take all the time and never give. Selfishness is poison to any relationship—on your plane or any other.

Younger souls constantly make this mistake. For example, younger siblings often talk for lengthy periods about themselves while asking their older brothers and sisters little about how they are doing. Most children and grandchildren don't learn until late in life to start asking their elders how they are doing and what they are thinking about. Only the most considerate and mature of younger souls thinks to ask its elders how it can return the energy it has been given.

People would be wise not to make this classic mistake with a messenger. We *have our own lives, our own projects, our own interests. Would it kill you to occasionally ask us how we are doing?*

This is important not so much because we need to be asked but because we want you to grow and mature to the point where you care enough to ask. When we see such growth, we feel a sense of accomplishment. This is part of our reward for the work we do with you.

Another thing that you can do is to offer to help us. We have our own projects. We absolutely love it when one of you is thoughtful enough to say, "What can I do to help you?"

Yes, but *how* exactly are we supposed to help you? Most of us can't even hear you. We have no idea what you want or what to do to help you.

That doesn't matter. The way to go about this is to first offer to help. Then, be quiet. Open your eyes and look around. Listen to the world around you. Those that have ears will hear.

Pay attention and persist. There will be signs—a phone call asking for a contribution, a letter in the mailbox, a person on the street—it could be anything. If you are paying attention and anticipating, you will know. Trust me: If you are paying attention, you will know. It's not that difficult.

[*Silence.*] Are there any other ways we can encourage your presence?

[Pause.] *Have you ever had a friend or relative who only called you or visited when there was a problem or need? How did that make you feel?*

I do know people like that. In fact, I probably act the same way myself sometimes.

True. That's just how children are.

Do you see me as a child?

We see all of you as children, and we love all of you no matter what you do. But we really wish you would call on us more when you are having a good time. You need to work on this. Don't just call us when you get in trouble—during the bad times. Don't act this way with any messenger. It is somewhat rude and inconsiderate.

Remember that we love joy and fun. Granted, we don't really need your help to have fun. It's just that it is polite and considerate to include us in the good times as well as the bad.

How should we do this exactly?

It's all done in consciousness. When things are going great, all you have to do is remember us. This simple act of awareness is greatly appreciated by your guardians, who will consider it a sign of spiritual maturity. Like good teachers everywhere, we like to see signs that our students are making progress. That is a major part of our reward for working with you.

When we need help, how should we ask you to help us? Is there a certain way that is better than others?

One of the most common mistakes people make in dealing with us is to ask for our help only with self-centered plans. It's perfectly normal to ask us to help with personal projects, up to a point. Everyone has certain projects and plans that are based around the self. But it is important for you to understand that you should always be looking outside of yourself, always trying to integrate your personal good with the greater good. Whenever you are involved in something that will benefit many, you automatically pull additional power from the Spirit. We are the agents of that power. We are the vehicles through which Spirit transmits itself into your lives.

Think of others. Look at what you are doing and continually ask yourself: Will this benefit anyone else? Will this contribute to the greater good? Such questions will expand your awareness beyond the boundaries of the self and will attract our presence and our help. I suggest you think of the Amish woman and her family and start practicing right now.

Chapter Five

J im begged me not to let him suffer. When I found the tumor in his lung, he took me aside and looked straight into my eyes. "You are my doctor. I'm counting on you," he said in a level voice. "Don't let me lie there for weeks slowly suffocating. Promise me."

What could I do? I promised him. Now I had to keep that promise.

It was no wonder he developed lung cancer. Jim was one of a handful of Americans who had been in Nagasaki right after the bomb was dropped. The army sent him in to document and photograph the destruction after the surrender. One cold winter day while he could still speak, I sat at his bedside and asked him what it was like there. "At ground zero," he said, "the ground had fused to glass." When I asked him about the people, he just looked away. He wouldn't say anything else.

Now he was lying in his bed comatose. The bomb had finally killed him too.

True to my word, I didn't let him suffer. I had a morphine drip going full blast. Not enough to euthanize him, but plenty enough to keep him out of pain. His wife had thanked me for this a dozen times already as she wandered in and out of his room in a state of anticipatory grief.

He took an amazingly long time to die. He lay there in bed day after day, his respirations barely perceptible. Nobody could believe his heart was still beating—it didn't seem physiologically possible. Finally, as I was doing morning rounds on the tenth day, he decided the time was right and, with a final agonizing breath, took leave of his earthly form.

It wasn't that bad, you know.

It looked just awful. I felt so bad for you.

With as much medicine as you gave me, I was out of my body several days ago. I just kind of hung around here watching things. Even though it was already over, it was harder to let go of that body than you might think. [Pause.] You know, you could have talked to me during the last few days. Why did you wait until now?

I didn't know. I didn't think to try until you had actually died.

There's no need for you to make that mistake again. Just because someone is in a coma doesn't mean they can't hear you. You should know better than that.

I'm sorry. I've always suspected that patients in that state could hear and feel at some level. It just feels a bit awkward talking to someone who is unconscious.

You don't have to talk. You know that too. Just know that they can commune with you. When you know in your heart they can hear, they can hear.

If people can hear, then why don't they remember this when they wake up?

Do you remember your dreams when you wake up? Do you remember the things that you hear at night when you sleep?

No. Very rarely.

Memory doesn't work in a coma like it does in normal waking consciousness. There is only the here and now in a coma. When you awake, your memory will be empty.

Talk to your patients, Doc. Always talk to them. Inside—in your heart. You know better. [Pause.] You know I feel a lot of love for my wife.

I know. And she knows too. She's doing remarkably well. You guys must have talked about this a lot in the last few months.

We talked about it for a long, long time. She knew I was at peace with this. I lived much longer than I ever thought possible. That bomb should have killed me long ago. There are others with me now. I am in good hands. [Pause.] I'm ready.

[Silence.] I am with you. Ask what you will.

You know, seeing all the pain, the disease, and the death that I do makes me wonder. When that Amish woman died and those eight kids were left without a mother, you said they planned things that way. I have a lot of questions about this. I keep seeing the same kind of notion in certain books that I have been reading—the notion that we create our own reality. Is this really true? I mean, part of me believes this, but another part of me has a lot of trouble with the concept.

Of course it's true.

[Silence.] Do we create our own reality, the basic structure of our lives, before we are born or after—while we are alive?

Both. Before you are born, you are allowed to set up some of the basic parameters of your life. Whether you will be a man or a woman, smart or dumb, tall or short, talented or ordinary—things like that.

You mean things that will be genetically determined?

Yes, but other things too.

Like what?

Like whether you will grow up rich or poor, in a modern country or an underdeveloped country, whether you will contract certain diseases or develop certain problems, whether you will find true love or not. All sorts of things that might be classified as "environmental factors."

If this were true, it would explain many difficult problems we see here on Earth, but I'm still having a problem. If we set all of this stuff up in advance, doesn't that mean we are locked into a certain fate, that we don't really have free will once we get here? If that is so, then how can you say that we create our own realities in this life? It sounds like they were already created before birth.

You get to set up some, but not all, of your basic parameters in advance if you want to. But I can assure you there is plenty of room to flow and change and create in and around these parameters.

What do you mean, "If you want to"? Not everyone plans things out in advance?

You know people. Do all of them plan things out in advance?

No. I suppose not. I know a lot of people who have very poor skills in this area.

It's like this. Some souls are very willful, very arrogant. They don't want to listen to anyone. They won't let us explain things to them. They won't let us help them set up a plan that makes sense for them, that will help them progress and evolve in an efficient, organized way once they take birth. They are like people who flop into college with little forethought and take courses in a rather haphazard and chaotic way.

There are a lot of things about this that still don't make sense to me. For example, if we get to set things up ourselves, why don't we all choose to be healthy, rich, and happy in this life? For that matter, why doesn't everybody choose to be talented, famous, and well loved?

Well, first of all, there aren't that many positions available in your system for "famous, well-loved people." Fame, by definition, means that you are that one in a million person that everybody else recognizes. You can't very well have ten million *"famous"* people on Earth. People couldn't pay attention to nearly that many famous people, and they would therefore not be famous. Do you see what I mean?

I guess that makes sense.

Besides, there is a huge waiting list for positions like that. Many, many people want to take birth as "famous, well-loved people" even though we rarely recommend it. Some of them are willing to wait in line for an amazingly long time to do so.

Are you saying anyone can take birth as a famous and well-loved person, or a very wealthy person, or a very talented person, or a very powerful person if they are willing to wait long enough?

No. There is more to it than that. You have to be qualified too.

How do you become qualified?

By laying the right groundwork, by taking the necessary prerequisite courses of study, as it were.

So if you want to be, say, a famous singer, you have to develop great talent as a singer before you take birth?

Not necessarily. It's more like you have to accumulate enough—how can I say this—"credits," I guess is as good a word as any. Then you can spend these credits in any way you see fit.

How do you get these credits?

There is only one way credits can be accumulated, and that is by selfless, loving thoughts and deeds.

So, if you are a very selfless, giving, generous, loving soul prior to birth and thereafter, you can accumulate a lot of credits and spend them to be anything you want?

Not anything. It is like winning tokens at an amusement park. When you go up to the counter to cash them in, you can only get a desired prize if it is being offered.

What did you mean when you said you don't recommend being a famous, well-loved person?

I mean it's not always good for you to be famous and well loved, or powerful, or wealthy, or beautiful, or exceptionally intelligent, or talented in the big scheme of things. Being the center of attention tends to make you feel like you are the center of the universe. This increases your sense of self-importance, which in turn leads you to undo all the selfless work you did to get there in the first place. People who experience fame also have great difficulty focusing on other individuals. They have a lot of trouble with intimacy and cooperating with others as equals.

Surely you are not implying that all exceptional people are self-centered, self-important jerks?

No. Of course not. Some are humble and very deep. After all, there have to be some exceptional people, some figures that others can look up to and imitate. It hasn't been set up so that it is completely impossible to be extraordinary and be a decent person at the same time. It's just that it is a very difficult act to pull off, that's all.

[Pause.] It sounds like the information you are giving me confirms the doctrine of reincarnation, that we come back over and over as different people here on Earth.

No, the doctrine of reincarnation is not exactly accurate. But neither is the notion that you go to an eternal heaven or hell and just sit there forever. [Laughter.] How would that serve the Creator's plans?

Look around you. The Creator recycles everything, everything. Infinite Intelligence is a very efficient, thoughtful, conservative force that wastes nothing. Waste is dumb and God isn't dumb. You know that, you have worked with this concept for several years now.

If we don't reincarnate and we aren't warehoused in an eternal heaven or hell, then what does happen? How does this work?

The problem with the concept of reincarnation is that it creates the false impression that a distinct "you" keeps coming back over and over. That is not the case. When "you" die, you are no longer "you." That term "you" ceases to have any meaning. "You" reemerge into the great light and your identity is no longer relevant. That is why we don't have much use for names here.

It's better to look at it like this: Something returns to continue the process of evolution that it began in previous lives but that something is an extension of God, not "you." Besides, there are an incredible number of worlds, and an incredible number of dimensions. The thing that returns, the "soul," I guess you could call it, doesn't necessarily return to Earth.

No offense, but Earth is almost negligible in the overall scheme of things. It is but a tiny subatomic particle in the whole, a place that lives for a relative "nano-second," to use one of your terms. This business about individual people returning to Earth over and over, climbing a tidy ladder of evolution from animal to human and finally enlightenment, is grossly oversimplified. It is much more fluid, much more diversified than that. It's hard to explain. Besides, the mechanism is a trivial matter. It doesn't really matter in a practical sense.

All that really matters is that you engage yourself in selfless, positive, generous action wherever you are right now. Forget about reincarnation and heaven and hell and all that. Worrying and arguing about concepts like those won't help you or anyone else in the slightest.

So there is definitely no eternal heaven and no eternal hell?

I didn't say that. I said you don't sit in one forever.

I don't get it.

If you want to believe in an eternal heaven or an eternal hell, then such a place is automatically created by your belief, and you are welcome to go there and experience "eternity." At least until you are tired of it. [Laughter.]

Hell exists all right, but there is no one hell. Actually, there are many, many hells. You humans create them constantly and descend into them all the time. You can create and inhabit any kind of awful place you want. That's your choice. [Laughter.] The funny thing is, all the people who use that word, "hell," automatically put one foot in it every time they think or say it.

Religions that dwell on such things cause so much needless pain. Why do you people think these kinds of things up?

People pay attention to books like the Bible and the Torah and the Koran that talk about this kind of traditional concept. They respect these books, have faith in them, and believe what they say. Some of them believe everything and take it all very literally. They believe these books are God's word.

Well, God spoke. But human beings listened, human beings wrote down what was said, human beings translated, rearranged, and retranslated what was originally said, and now look what you've got. These are beautiful books, and we love them as much as you, but you wrote them, not us. You know what is a lot healthier, a lot more effective than reading about what somebody else thinks about the Spirit?

Well?

Listening to Spirit yourself. This is much safer, much more accurate. The process of evolution is designed to bring everyone to the state of direct contact in time.

[*Silence.*] Do you mind if I ask you a few more questions about this business of creating our own realities?

It's a confusing concept, isn't it, at least from your side?

That is putting it mildly. The fact is, I think all kinds of thoughts, and I rarely see any of them take form. Some do, I will admit that, but others never manifest. For example, for a few years when I was a small boy, I had all kinds of hypochondriacal thoughts—very passionate clear visualizations about certain diseases that I thought I was going to contract. Lots of doctors have these when they're young. It's common.

But these thoughts never came true. That's hard to understand because my worries filled all the criteria for viable thought forms: They were vivid, persistent, and charged with deeply felt emotions. And yet they never came to pass. How do you explain that?

Spirit built several safety factors into the creative process to help limit the damage people cause themselves. The main safety factor is a delay effect—when you think a thought there is an automatic delay before it takes shape. If not for this delay, human beings would self-destruct about ten minutes after taking birth. Do you have any idea what kinds of things go through your mind when you wake up as a tiny helpless infant on the hard, cold, physical plane? Don't remember, do you?

No.

Things like "I'm blind! I'm freezing! I'm dying!" Now, how would it work if things were set up so that these thoughts manifested immediately as reality?

[Laughter.] Not well.

Changing your reality by changing the way you think is like feeding and watering a tree. Let's say you have a tree in your yard that is growing poorly. You decide to start paying attention to this problem and begin watering and fertilizing the tree so that it will thrive. The first day you go outside, turn the hose on, and give the tree a good watering along with a little fertilizer. What do you then see?

Nothing, I guess. The tree isn't going to have any noticeable improvement for a long time.

Does that mean you should stop watering and fertilizing the tree? Of course not. You know that this program will ultimately result in improvement if you persist. So, every few days, with great consistency, you continue to water the tree. Within a few weeks you begin to notice subtle changes. Within a few years, you have a beautiful, lush tree.

So there is no doubt that thinking better thoughts will result in a better reality? You are absolutely sure about this?

[Laughter.] *Of course I'm sure. Your reality is a fluid, malleable thing. It responds to your thoughts—reflects your thoughts—perfectly. This delay thing will give you fits, though, if you don't understand it. When you start to change the quality of your thoughts and visualizations, you have to know what to expect* in the way of results. The difficult, stubborn problems you are currently facing will loosen and break apart slowly like a frozen river thawing in the springtime. Does a frozen river thaw all at once?

No.

Neither will your reality. At first you will have a few warm days and the surface will soften ever so slightly. Then the weather will turn cold again and everything will freeze. It will look like all your progress has been lost. Then, slowly but very surely, there will be more and more warm days. The ice will soften and thin. A few cracks will appear here, a patch will open up there to reveal running water beneath.

Finally, one day when you least expect it, the ice will break apart and huge chunks will suddenly let loose and float away downstream. You just have to keep the sun shining on that ice, day after day, and everything will be okay. Even the most impossible situations can become fluid if you persist.

All situations? This works for any problem?

Not every problem. You set some things up in advance in such a way that they will occur no matter what you think.

[Silence.] I still see problems with this notion. One of the things that has always troubled me about the idea that we create our own reality is that I see things happening to me and around me that I never thought about. In fact, most of the things that have manifested in my life I never thought about at all. Don't some things just happen randomly? How does all this garbage end up in my life?

It's all there in the Bible. I use that book as an example because you have a Judeo-Christian upbringing and are familiar with common biblical stories and parables. It has all been explained in great detail. You just can't see it.

Where?

Well, to begin with you have the story of Adam and Eve and the Garden of Eden.

So you're confirming that isn't a literal account of something that really happened.

Oh, come on, you know better than that. It's much deeper. It's a metaphor, and everything in the story symbolizes something else. What do you think the garden represents in the story?

The world? Reality?

It's much bigger. The garden is God. Reality is God. Everything happens within God. Everything is living and growing in God, which is just another name for this whole thing, this whole universe, this infinite flowing field of possibility and potential that stretches everywhere around us—all of us. Think about it: What is a garden exactly?

It's a place where you grow things.

And how do you grow things?

You plant seeds, water them, cultivate them, and then they more or less grow automatically.

Precisely. And what are the seeds and plants in the Garden of Eden?

[Pause.] Thoughts?

Right. You have had many gardens in real life. Remember what happens when you plant seeds? What is it really like to raise plants from seeds?

You put seeds in the ground. Then, after a delay like the one you just told me about, they sprout and grow. What are you getting at?

But what comes up with the seeds? When you were younger and had your garden in that nice black topsoil, what came up with your seeds?

Weeds, I guess. What's your point?

That's where your garbage comes from. Remember the Parable of the Tares that Jesus talked about?

Wasn't that the one where a farmer planted his crops in a field? Then, while he slept, an enemy came and sowed tares, which are basically weeds?

That's the one. And what happened when the crops came up?

They were all tangled up with weeds.

Who do you think the "enemy" is in this story?

The devil, I suppose.

Nonsense, there is no devil. You know that.

Then I don't know. You tell me.

The enemy is the ego, the self. Look at the wording of that parable very closely. What do you think "the enemy came while he slept" means? What happens when you sleep? Technically now. You're a doctor. You know about these things. What really happens during sleep?

The conscious mind relaxes to the point where it stops functioning, and you go into a deep state of relaxation.

Is that it? Is that all?

No. Usually the subconscious takes over and begins to dream.

Keep going. What are dreams?

Chaotic sequences of thoughts and images that float up out of the subconscious.

It's right there in front of you. Think about it.

[Pause.] You mean, the subconscious mind is the enemy that sows the weed seeds?

Think it through.

That makes sense in a lot of ways. The subconscious mind is extremely vast and very powerful. If you try to sow a few beneficial thoughts at the conscious level, your subconscious mind will still be working away thinking who knows what.

Right. Things like "Oh, no. I'm just not sure. Dad always told me I wasn't that smart. I just know I'm going to fail. I wonder what will ever happen to me"—all kinds of chaotic, negative, and at best vague thought forms. Is it any wonder you see chaotic, negative, and vague circumstances manifest in your life? Remember the Parable of the Sower?

Yes. A sower goes out and sows a bunch of seeds. Some fall on the rocks, some in shallow soil, and some on fertile soil. The ones that fall on fertile soil grow but the others die. What has that got to do with it? Jesus was talking about spreading the word of God. Some of the word falls on bad people, some on good people. The word that falls on the good people takes root and grows within them.

Not necessarily. That was the great thing about Jesus. He was really smart. Way, way smarter than people give him credit for. People don't realize it, but he was a genius. Some of his parables had three or four levels of meaning. If you look at that parable hard and translate it very carefully, you will see that it doesn't say a sower went out and sowed "his" seed, it really says a sower went out and sowed "the seed of himself." The word for "self" is the Greek autos. Check the original Greek if you don't believe me. Now, what are the seeds of someone's self?

I know what you're going to say. They're a person's thoughts and dreams and aspirations?

Actually, Jesus explains exactly what the seeds are. When he is asked to explain this parable a few verses later, he says that the seeds are the "word of the kingdom." Pay careful attention to the exact words that are used. Keep probing: What is the kingdom?

Heaven?

Where is heaven?

He said it was inside us.

And what does that say about heaven?

[Pause.] That it is a state of consciousness?

And what is a state of consciousness?

A collection of thoughts, I guess.

So what is the "word of the kingdom"?

Thoughts about heaven?

Keep going. What would those be like?

They would be good thoughts, really good thoughts.

Right. Now, keep looking at the parable, but think of the seeds the sower is sowing as thoughts about heaven—very elevated, positive, creative, loving, beneficial thoughts. What happens when these thoughts fall on poor soil?

They die. I guess that's what happens when they stay at the level of the self, the ego.

Good. What happens when they fall on fertile soil, in the garden of pure potential, as it were—in the part of the greater self that is one with God, one with the garden?

They take root and bear fruit according to the parable—some one hundredfold.

Right. Just like in a real garden. You plant one seed and the mature plant brings forth a hundred more. What Jesus said is that the seed that dies is the man who hears the word but "hath not root in himself." Someone who doesn't have a root in himself is someone who has no awareness of his real nature, someone who has no conscious contact with the wellspring of infinite power and intelligence deep inside.

[*Silence.*] All right. I understand about the weeds now, but I have one more question. Even when I take away the subconscious thoughts I've sown in this lifetime, I'm still left with some issues I can't explain. Like why I was born into a good family, why I was short for my age in grade school, things like that. Neither my conscious thoughts nor my subconscious thoughts can explain some things.

I already told you. Some of the things that sprout up from the garden around you are the result of seeds you sowed in the past. In your garden this year—did anything come up that you didn't plant this year?

Yes. Several plants, a large onion and two tomatoes, sprouted from seeds that were left in the soil last fall.

There is nothing to say you can't sow seeds before you are born into your current life. You don't remember sowing them, but make no mistake, you sowed them all right. You created all of your life.

It's kind of frightening when you think about it.

It is very challenging, very scary in a lot of ways. In fact, this is why so many people have trouble accepting the whole concept of self-created reality, why they get so angry and indignant about it. It's not so much that it disagrees with their personal metaphysics. A lot of it is that they find it extremely frightening. They can't face it.

If it's true, the implications are very threatening. It means that they are responsible for their own problems and for fixing them as well. It means they can't blame some imaginary devil for their woes. They can't blame God either. They can't blame other people, or the government, or some political party, and they can't explain their circumstances on random bad luck.

You have to understand. Some of the things that happen in people's lives are quite horrible. A lot of souls just aren't ready to see that they are causing these things to happen themselves. They have so little control over their thought processes and their subconscious minds are so loaded with negative garbage that if they were to suddenly and fully realize that all of their chaotic and fearful thoughts were being sown into an incredibly fertile soil and would ultimately bear fruit, they would go insane knowing they were totally out of control. So they go into denial about the whole process and get very emotional and irrational when the issue is raised. The idea that some kind of external "devil" is responsible is much more convenient and reassuring by comparison.

Chapter Six

The ambulance crew wheeled Bill H. through the doors of the ER at three a.m. Two disheveled and eccentric friends hovered by his bedside. Although dirty and dressed in shabby, ill-fitting clothing, this peculiar pair was nonetheless likeable and strangely familiar. Speaking with them evoked a curious sensation of déjà vu, which I shrugged off at the time as insignificant.

The two companions told me they believed Bill had taken about one hundred Tylenol and fifty or sixty Dilaudid, a potent narcotic. They found the empty bottles on his nightstand when they went over to check on him. Why they suddenly decided to go over at midnight was unclear. Obviously Bill had not called them.

They hesitated before calling 911, and I couldn't blame them. Bill had been dying from AIDS for over a year. He should have died a month or two previously, but his heart and lungs kept pumping away as if they simply didn't know any better. It was hard to believe anyone could be this sick and still be alive. When I examined him, his body looked like it was dissolving. His pain must have been horrible in the previous months.

One of the nurses knew the patient and had watched him struggle with his disease for the last few years. Bill had apparently prayed in vain to be healed and had felt bad that God had not answered his urgent requests for assistance. He had grown bitter in the end.

It was too late to save him. The medications had long since been ingested and absorbed, so pumping his stomach would have no benefit. Besides, he had left clear instructions—typed and notarized on his medical chart—that no extraordinary measures be taken if he fell into a coma. As I stood there contemplating my next move, I heard his death rattle and he suddenly passed away. Nobody even looked at the crash cart. I turned around but his companions had vanished. I learned later that no one had ever seen them before.

Who were those two people? Where did they go?

Can't you guess?

This doesn't make any sense. Why didn't you simply let this guy die at home? Why did you go to all the trouble to get him all the way over here and then have him die ten minutes later?

It has nothing to do with him. He is perfectly fine. He was out of his body and at peace with his transition hours ago. It has to do with you.

Meaning?

Meaning we know you have questions and need to speak with us. We thought this would help get things moving. Bill said he didn't mind, he was leaving anyway. It didn't matter to him a bit one way or the other. So it was arranged that he die in front of you to stimulate your spiritual search.

What are you anyway? The angel of death? You must be to keep showing up at these times.

[Laughter.] *Oh, that has such a terrible sound to it.* [Pause.] *Let's just say you can think of me as an "evolution messenger." Death is only one of the many processes of evolution I oversee.*

Are you sure he's okay? Can I do anything more for him?

Your prayers as he made the final transition were enough for you. Now it is best that you turn your attention back to your questions. Bill would be the first to agree. He's doing beautifully now.

[Pause.] I will admit that I am still having problems with the information you have given me. I've considered everything you've told me so far. In a lot of ways it all sounds very reasonable, very convincing. But the more I think about it, the more there seems to be some glaring inconsistencies in your information.

[Laughing.] *Go ahead.*

The most troublesome problem I'm having concerns the relationship between free will and divine will. You told me before that messengers are like God's fingers, that God uses you to adjust and correct the delicate chains of cause and effect that define people's lives. Is that true?

Yes.

But you also told me that people are allowed to create their own reality, that they set things up for themselves. Is that also true?

Yes.

Well, these two notions seem to be entirely incompatible. Which is it? Does God adjust and correct our lives, or do we create them ourselves? It seems to me you can't have it both ways.

[Laughter.] *True. Not the way you are thinking about it. The problem is that you are making a gigantic and entirely erroneous assumption. This assumption causes you, and almost everyone else for that matter, a vast amount of confusion and grief.*

So, what is this "erroneous assumption"?

You assume that you and God are two different beings and have two different agendas. This is simply not the case.

Are you saying that I am in fact God?

[Great laughter.] *Of course!*

Why is that funny?

It's funny to hear God asking in that kind of suspicious, accusatory tone if he is in fact God. Only you would set up such a fascinating joke on yourself.

[*Silence.*] You hear this all the time. I mean, it's a theme that seems to run through many of the major religions: That our true self is one with the divine self. However, in reality—everyday, concrete, practical, down-to-Earth reality—it doesn't work that way at all. We are just people, plain and simple. If we are God, we certainly don't know it. And because we aren't aware of it we are not, for all practical purposes, God. It may be true at some high philosophical level, but it's nothing more than a nice metaphysical concept for ordinary people.

If you say so. [Laughter.]

[*Silence.*] You're not going to respond?

What am I supposed to say? It sounds like you have already decided what is true and closed your mind.

[*Pause.*] Let's try this another way. Let me ask you this: Let's say a human being has a problem. Let's say, for example, a person learns he is in mortal danger. He prays to God with all his might. His faith is genuine and very strong. What happens? Do messengers become involved at this point? Does God send you in to help the situation? If so, doesn't that mean the person is no longer creating his own reality?

You still don't understand. We are you, the real you. If we get involved—and you should make no mistake about it, we do get involved in your lives—we do so as extensions of your own will. But that's just it, way down deep, your will and God's will are one and the same. While you are down there in that guise playing that role, you are not aware of this, but it is nonetheless true.

When you think a thought or pray a prayer—prayer being a kind of thought—that thought goes out into the universe and begins to take form. You, Spirit, and all of Spirit's messengers and agents, all of us are connected together in one milieu, one gigantic coordinated field of consciousness.

This field of consciousness is like a fertile garden. Thoughts planted in its soil germinate and grow into real concrete circumstances. All of us—humans, messengers, and Infinite Intelligence—are the seeds, the garden, and the gardener, simultaneously.

[Laughter.] It's very hard to explain to a human, but that's how it is set up. That is how Spirit has constructed itself so that it can constantly generate new and different realities, realities that keep growing and evolving.

[Pause.] Another way of looking at it is that messengers don't answer your prayers, we are your prayers. We are living, fluid forms of light that emanate from mind. We respond to God's mind and to yours. Again, they are one and the same.

This is very difficult to explain. A lot of it has to do with the language barrier. Here's an idea: Give me an example and I'll show you how this works.

Okay. Let's say I learn that I have cancer or AIDS, like this guy who just died. I get really concerned. I'm terrified. I start to pray. I ask God to take the cancer away so that I can live. I am not so much concerned for myself as I am for my family. If I die they will be plunged into terrible grief, perhaps poverty. My pleas for help are in every way reasonable.

This is a situation that comes up a lot. I see it all the time as a doctor: People having horrible medical problems—good people, decent people, people with a great deal of faith and trust in God. They pray, their family prays, sometimes their whole church prays. And yet they often die anyway. This is reality and it doesn't seem to jibe at all with what you are saying.

[Softly.] But it does. You just can't see it. [Pause.] If a person gets cancer, would you agree that it is possible that the person has created this situation?

[Grudgingly.] I guess it's possible.

Would you also agree that it is possible, knowing what you know, that this situation was set up in advance, perhaps before the person was born? Would you agree that it is possible that the AIDS or the cancer is a kind of "course" designed by the person himself to help him learn certain specific useful things?

It's possible. But you are still not answering my question. Why aren't the person's prayers answered?

Let's go back to the beginning, before the person was born. Typically, a person who decides to set up his life so that he has cancer has a very good reason for doing so—this is not something that is done lightly. Generally speaking, such a person feels that the lessons that will be mastered are extremely important, so important that he is willing, even eager, to commit to the pain involved.

He is counseled. Beings of light, beings with enormous wisdom and compassion, take him aside. They inform him of the consequences involved in his decision. They tell him that the pain will be terrible, the terror intense and prolonged. Wisely, they make him wait a long time so that he doesn't commit hastily.

But he persists. The more he thinks about it, the more he realizes that passing through the veil, losing the knowledge of his true identity as a facet of God, and going through the drama of the disease process will help him get where he longs to go in consciousness. Where he longs to go is back to the Spirit. He wants to realize with ever greater clarity and certainty that he is in fact God.

He begs for this privilege. He waits in line to demonstrate his conviction. And he insists—insists, mind you—that he be locked into this situation. He leaves explicit instructions that we are not to alter the situation in the slightest. No matter how much he pleads and begs, he tells us, we are not to intervene.

Finally, he is allowed to take birth and the day comes that the cancer begins to unfold. As soon as he learns of it, he becomes terrified. He can't remember that he is God, that he is everything, that he is immortal. So he straightaway starts begging us to take the cancer away.

Now, you tell me, what are we supposed to do? After all he has been through setting this up, completing all the prerequisites, waiting in line, demonstrating his conviction, waiting some more, then going to all of the trouble involved in taking birth, and growing up, and all the rest—what are we supposed to do? Do you expect us to immediately swoop in and dismantle the whole intricate setup? If we do, we will cure the cancer but in effect ruin his whole life. That would be quite counterproductive and destructive. Furthermore, it would be utterly unethical.

If it is really the way you say it is, then I guess it wouldn't make any sense to take the cancer away. But why, in other cases, do diseases and other misfortunes go away when people pray?

There are clearly cases where certain "incurable" diseases are resolved with the aid of prayer. I am absolutely convinced of that. I've seen it happen.

Not all "misfortunes" are locked in at the outset. Some people choose to have situations that are flexible, changeable. The reasons for this vary. Suffice it to say that there are useful lessons to be learned while undergoing diseases and other misfortunes that are locked in and useful lessons to be learned while undergoing such states that are not locked in. There are valuable lessons to be learned from having prayers answered and from having prayers unanswered. Surely you can see that.

But I still don't understand why anyone in their right mind would beg and plead to have cancer or AIDS, like this guy that just died, or any other terrible misfortune. I have personally experienced situations that were so painful that I cursed God. I got very angry. "Why," I asked, "would you ever let me get myself into such a situation—for any reason?" There is absolutely no excuse for some of these things. I just don't believe that people would ever be so stupid as to knowingly set up some of the horrible and excruciatingly painful tragedies they undergo.

This still doesn't make any sense. There has to be an easier way.

I mean, I can see why suffering can lead to growth and why we might consent to it—even *request* it in certain circumstances—but I don't see why it has to be as *bad* as it is. The suffering I see here on Earth seems quite excessive.

Do you remember when you finally decided you wanted to go to go back to school to get your premedical training?

Sure I remember.

Do you remember the curriculum you set up for yourself?

Yes.

How did you set it up?

I wanted to get through it as quickly as possible, I will admit that. So I signed up to take twice as many courses per semester as was recommended.

Did your adviser say anything?

Oh, yes. She told me not to do it—not to get myself into that kind of a situation.

Did you do it, anyway?

Yes.

Did you have to twist her arm to cosign your schedule?

In effect, yes. In fact, I was somewhat of a pain about it.

Was it painful to go through all those courses at the same time?

I must admit it was pretty bad. Horrible, in fact.

Did you bail out in the middle?

No, I went through it anyway. Very few people bailed out, actually.

Are you glad you did it?

I suppose. In retrospect, yes. I got the hard part out of the way very quickly.

Did you learn what you needed to learn?

Yes.

Did you get where you wanted to go?

Yes.

Then what's the problem? Don't you see how it works yet? The reason it gets so bad down there is because almost all of you that take birth on Earth are very intense souls. You are real go-getters. Very impressive, really. Most of you want to progress very, very quickly. I'm telling you, you set these things up and you lock yourselves in.

We put you all together on one planet so that you would all have certain intense experiences available to you that would satisfy your requests. It's a matter of efficiency. Spirit is unbelievably efficient. It sets up certain places that can satisfy the requests of billions of souls at a time.

[Pause.] I'm still not a hundred percent clear about this. Let's say I am a soul over on your side. You are in heaven, right?

That is your word for it.

Heaven is a really great place, right? I would assume it is very pleasant to be there.

It's not really a "place." I've told you that. It is a state of consciousness— a fluid, ever-changing, dynamic process. Heaven is a verb, not a noun.

That's just semantics. What I'm getting at is this: If I am a soul over there and experiencing bliss and all, why would I want to leave—for any reason? I don't understand that at all.

Most of us don't want to leave. Although time, as such, does not exist here, you could say for the purposes of conversation that we stay here a long, long time. But most of us eventually get to a point where we realize that we want to learn and experience certain things. Like you, we have a natural desire to improve ourselves. All extensions of Spirit, all creatures, are like Spirit. We are all made in the image of God, and God has an incredibly pronounced tendency to progress, to create, to learn, and to evolve.

Some of the things we need to learn can only be learned while in a body, a body that feels pleasure and pain. Some of the things we have to learn about faith and love and hope and inner strength and acceptance can only be accomplished while in a state of relative ignorance—while disguised as a being that can't remember what it really is. I don't know how to explain it to you any better than that.

So we don't actually have to be here?

Of course not. I've tried to tell you. You beg to be there.

[Silence.] So how do you, how do messengers, think of us? How do you view us from your vantage point as we slog away down here?

This may surprise you, but we often view you with envy. Since many of us are waiting to take form there, we see you as very privileged, exalted beings in most cases. I'll use the medical school example again to show you how this is. Do you remember when you were waiting to be accepted to medical school?

How could I forget?

Do you remember visiting there when you were interviewing?

Of course.

Remember how you looked at all those students walking around in their white jackets and scrub suits?

I thought they were practically like gods at the time. I was so envious.

But you knew they were going through all kinds of stressful and painful experiences, didn't you?

Yes.

But you still looked at them with envy even though your life as an undergrad was less stressful by comparison?

Yes, I suppose I did.

That's how we see you sometimes. Sure, it's great here. But feeling great isn't all there is. All the creatures of the universe are made in Spirit's image. So we all possess the desire to grow and create new realities just like the Creator. Some messengers are extremely eager to learn. They will do anything, anything to go through the kind of intense "boot camp" you find yourselves in down there.

[*Silence.*] You said a while ago that there are some situations that are locked in and some that are not.

Right.

One thing I have been wondering about is this: If a messenger does respond to a thought form such as a prayer, how exactly does the messenger respond?

Remember that we are, in essence, extensions of your own thoughts. Deep down inside you is a place where you are connected to the Spirit, one with the Spirit. In that place we are also one with you. When you pray correctly, that prayer—how shall I say this—"becomes" a messenger. True prayers are direct extensions of the Divine mind. These extensions live—they germinate, they grow, they take form, and they change things.

You mean when a prayer is uttered, a brand-new messenger is formed just to answer that prayer?

Not exactly. We are already there inside you. The light and all of its rays are shining within your true self all of the time. We simply move in response to your thoughts. It's part of our job, I guess you could say.

How does this really look, I mean, to you: How does this look from your side?

We see human beings as cocoons of light and energy. These cocoons are like tiny buds extending from the great light that is God. When a human being prays a prayer, it is as though a beam of light emerges from this cocoon like a flame. This flame radiates outward. It can travel and have remote effects. If it is sustained by persistent thoughts, it can solidify and eventually take form on the material plane.

This is so hard for me to imagine. I keep wanting to think of messengers as people, distinct separate entities that have their own lives.

We are distinct and we do have our own lives. But we can also merge—with each other and with you. We are not, like humans, confined to one form. As you were told, we are like the flames of a candle—fluid, light, and capable of assuming any form, anywhere.

We enable your prayers to be carried out by becoming those prayers. But when the task has been completed we merge back into our own light. This is hard to explain to a person on your plane. There are no human words for what we do. [Pause.] Let me try this in a different way. When you speak into a telephone, what happens?

My voice is converted into electronic impulses that pass over a wire. When they reach a receiver, they are converted back into sound waves.

The way we respond to prayers is something like this. When you pray, we pick up your thoughts, become your thoughts—which are as rays of light. We project out from your being and carry your thought impulses to their destination. When we arrive, we transform ourselves into the appropriate form to answer the prayer.

[Silence.] That sounds so complicated—so difficult. Isn't that a lot of trouble for you?

When you reach your hand out and grab a glass of water, many complex process occur. Hundreds of thousands of cells have to be coordinated and mobilized. Chemical bonds between billions of molecules have to be altered and rearranged in an extremely precise manner. That sounds complicated and difficult too. But do you consider the act of grabbing the glass of water difficult?

No.

It's the same with us. The whole process is quite effortless and natural even though a step-by-step breakdown of the mechanism makes it sound elaborate.

I'm having other problems.

Go ahead.

If everybody creates their own reality, what effects do the prayers of one person have upon another? If a friend or loved one is having a problem and I pray that this problem is eased, and you help me alter that person's reality so that the problem is improved, doesn't that take away the person's ability to create their own reality? Isn't this a contradiction?

If it worked that way, then yes, it would be a contradiction. But it's not quite that simple.

Are you saying that prayer, prayer for another, has no effect, that it is basically futile?

I didn't say that. Prayers can have enormously positive effects on others. It's just that they have to meet certain criteria to be successful.

What are the criteria?

For a prayer to help another person it must be properly framed. Generally speaking, it cannot request specific changes in another, however beneficial those changes might seem to the person sending the prayer.

The energy of prayer is not unlike the energy of money. Money on your plane is a symbol for time and energy. Time and energy are converted into the symbol of money so that they can be conveniently and effectively transferred. Prayer converts your personal energy into a kind of universal currency that we can use to help another person. But we must be left to spend the energy of prayer in any way we see fit. Only Spirit has the wisdom and the vantage point necessary to decide how to truly benefit another.

Some of the well-intended things you pray for another are actually harmful. For example, if you prayed to take another person's disease away, you might actually hurt that person. As I just tried to explain, some diseases and tragedies have been carefully and painstakingly set up by the person involved to provide them with an opportunity to accomplish major spiritual growth. If you took the situation away, you would ruin a great deal of careful planning. Can you see how destructive this would be? Who are you to assume you know what is truly best for another?

It is better, far better, to simply pray "God, help this person. Send them love and understanding and grace."

Send your care and your concern to those you seek to help, but keep things general. Send them a visualized gift of light if you wish. This will convert your attention into the currency of Spirit. Give this gift freely with no strings attached and let us spend it in the way we see fit.

[*Long pause.*] One more thing: You said that some of the situations we experience are not locked in, while others are. If I am to understand you correctly, this means that we can use prayer or visualization to reverse the situations that are *not* locked in but cannot use such techniques to reverse the ones that *are* locked in. Is that correct?

Essentially, yes.

Then sometimes when we pray or visualize passionately and diligently, we are wasting our time. What I want to know is, how can we know if a given situation has been locked in or if it hasn't? That seems very tricky to me. Is there in fact some way we can figure this out when we are trying to cope with a difficult problem?

There are ways, yes. [*Pause.*] *Do you know what the Serenity Prayer is?*

Sure. Everybody knows that. It's the prayer the Twelve Step groups use—you know, Alcoholics Anonymous, Overeaters Anonymous—those groups.

So? What does it say?

It says "God grant me the serenity to accept the things I cannot change, the courage to change the things I can, and the wisdom to know the difference."

That is the crux of the matter. You have to be able to accept the locked-in situations. We can't change these things for you because you have absolutely forbidden us to change them. But we can help you accept these things. We can help you with your reaction to these things. Let me ask you this: When you accept something that seems inevitable, what happens? What goes on in your mind?

It's hard to describe. Your mind sort of relaxes and gives up. You stop resisting and let go.

Right. And that is exactly what you design some situations to do, to force you to the point where you give up self-control. Remember, I said that you set your life up so that you are forced to go through certain painful things and that these experiences are designed to get you to a certain state of consciousness?

Yes.

The state you are trying to achieve in many of these circumstances is a state of acceptance. The state of acceptance is one of the highest forms of consciousness possible. Reaching this state is true evolution and brings you very close to Spirit. This is why when you finally accept something difficult, your life often starts to improve. You've gotten where you need to go, so the situation that's driving you to reach the state of acceptance is no longer necessary and begins to fall away.

Can you actually help us accept something? Can you help us with our internal states of mind?

Remember, we are your mind, we are your thoughts, we are your prayers. You, messengers, and God are all together, so yes, of course we can help you with acceptance. This is one of our very favorite tasks, actually. Like I say, acceptance is a highly evolved state.

[Pause.] And the "wisdom to know the difference"—you can help us with that too?

Look at the prayer carefully. When you pray the Serenity Prayer, you are asking God to grant you a certain piece of wisdom, to allow you to understand something. You are asking Spirit to allow you to perceive the true essence of a situation, to know whether it has been locked in or whether it can still be altered. Since Spirit knows whether a situation is locked in or not—Spirit knows everything—you can know this because Spirit is right there inside you.

The knowledge of whether something can be changed or not is never restricted. It has been set up so that human beings can always access this information. All they have to do is ask. But if your inner voice tells you that something can't be changed, you have to pay attention to it and believe it. Then you have to accept the truth and let go. That's the hard part. But that too is within everyone's reach.

[Pause.] And what are we to do if we ask for the wisdom to know the difference but are still confused? That seems to happen a lot.

[Laughter.] *That's easy. Just remember this cardinal rule: Whenever you are in doubt, accept, and release the situation into God's hands. Acceptance should always be your default mode when you're not sure how to proceed.*

From now on, use confusion to your advantage. If it persists, recognize it as an automatic signal that indicates a situation cannot be changed.

Chapter Seven

Leonard's death at the age of forty-five caught everyone by surprise. He was a brilliant classical musician, a Grammy winner known around the world for his virtuosity and creativity. His sudden passing rocked the musical world.

His wife, an old friend, had called me several days earlier from London to consult with me. While composing at the piano, Leonard had experienced a sudden bout of severe pain and weakness. After a brief workup in the emergency room, doctors concluded his appendix was to blame and removed it in an uneventful operation. All seemed well and he was soon scheduled to be released.

Then something terrible happened. As he was preparing to leave the hospital, his symptoms suddenly returned—a piercing pain in his chest and abdomen accompanied by severe weakness and shortness of breath. His wife rushed to the nurse's station for help, but she was told the pain was normal and would resolve soon. It didn't work. He worsened dramatically in the next hour while his wife, now frantic, begged his doctors to do something.

The resident on call finally decided to take the situation seriously, but it was too little, too late. Leonard arrested in his room, and prolonged attempts to resuscitate him failed. The autopsy later revealed that he had died as the result of a ruptured aortic aneurysm.

His wife was plunged into a grief of unspeakable depth. Nearly inseparable, they loved each with great intensity and devotion. I couldn't imagine her living without him. The next morning I flew to New York to help her arrange the funeral.

During my stay, I slept in the great musician's studio, which doubled as the guest bedroom. The atmosphere there was indescribable. All his instruments were arrayed just as he had left them. In that room once filled with soaring music, the deafening silence was profound.

It was obvious that Leonard had not moved on just yet. I couldn't blame him. His death was so abrupt and unexpected. He needed some time to get used to things. I could feel him in the house, hovering near his wife, trying to get oriented, trying to understand what was happening to him, trying to say good-bye, trying to accept. Although his presence was very intense, I couldn't hear him. But I did hear something else. Other beings were present, including my familiar messenger. Old and very wise, they were there to help Leonard make the transition.

Is he going to be okay?

Of course. Everyone is taken care of during this process. There is nothing to fear. You know that.

I really don't understand this at all. He was in the prime of his life. He had a long career ahead of him. He and his wife were so in love. Now look at her. She's in agony. Why must this be so? [*Angrily.*] Is this really necessary?

They obviously thought so.

By "they," you mean Leonard and his wife?

Think it through, knowing what you know.

I know, I know. You're going to tell me they planned it this way. But that really doesn't help us a whole lot right now, does it?

I'm sorry you're upset. But you plan these things yourself. You know that.

Why, though? Why would they do such a crazy thing?

Start with his wife. [Softly.] *Ask yourself: Is she the kind of person who would willingly go through a course of suffering if it would deepen her soul?*

Oh, yes. She has a long history of that.

She and Leonard have known each other—how shall I say it—for a long, long time.

You mean they knew each other in previous lives here?

I didn't say that. As we have told you, it's not that simple, not that tidy. Suffice it to say that they, like all other human beings, existed before—long before they were born on Earth. In these existences they formed an extremely strong bond. Before they came here, they decided to meet each other late in life, fall deeply in love, and then separate temporarily in this manner.

[Silence.] Why him? Why did he go first?

That's easy: She was much stronger. He would have fallen apart at the seams if she had gone first. It was better this way. Actually, she insisted he go first and he agreed that this was best for all concerned. Quite touching, really. It was incredibly considerate of her, and amazingly courageous. She knew what she was getting into and did it anyway for the sake of their relationship. She loves him that much. Besides, his work is done. His music has actually changed the entire planet in a very specific way.

So they'll be together again?

Do you really think Infinite Intelligence would just throw away a bond of love that strong after nurturing it along for eons? Now that would be something that wouldn't make sense.

Will they be together again as husband and wife?

Those are human words, human concepts. You can't continue to be so anthropomorphic and expect to understand how things work in the cosmic scheme of things. There are other ways to be together…much bigger ways.

So he won't necessarily be a man and she won't necessarily be a woman?

[Laughing.] *Are you asking us to predict the future?*

No, of course not. Nothing specific. I just want to understand the general process.

Let's just say they will be whatever they feel is most appropriate to help them learn what they want to learn. There are many other ways to be besides male and female. Those are earthly ways to manifest and fairly limited in their depth and scope.

[*Silence.*] Why do we have it this way in the first place—with different sexes, I mean? What is sex all about, anyway? What's really going on in these relationships?

[Laughter.] *Sex is a process human beings use to grow through specific problems.* [Pause.] *As we told you, souls here flow like energy, like light. We merge in and out of the great light and in and out of one another at times.*

Normally this is a very graceful, effortless process. But some souls have problems in this area. They have difficulties—how shall I say it—flowing into and through other souls, and then back out again. They experience friction and attachment and occasionally get stuck.

As I said, this is normally an effortless process, but it must still be perfected through practice. Swimming and riding a bicycle are effortless too, but before they become effortless these skills must be learned.

Souls here that wish to learn more about effortless merging and unmerging construct special courses they will undergo on Earth. These courses are designed to perfect their skills. Sex is often a part of these courses.

Are you saying messengers have sex of some kind? That sounds very irreverent somehow—pure blasphemy.

[Laughter.] *No. Of course not. Sex is something beings with physical bodies do. It is a very limited and rudimentary form of union. It is a kind of elementary exercise, like the exercises a novice musician practices. Only when the scales and arpeggios are mastered and become second nature after years of practice can beautiful and complex music flow effortlessly from the musician.*

It seems somewhat cavalier to reduce love to a simple "elementary" exercise.

It is far from simple for you. The relationship two beings may have on your plane can be extraordinarily complex. There are physical components, emotional components, mental components, and spiritual components involved in love. Further, there are a great variety of ways these various components can interact. To flow perfectly with other beings of light on our plane, all of the possible configurations must eventually be mastered.

[Pause.] *A lot of it has to do with etiquette. Much of what you go through in this area is to teach you consideration for others. The essence of our merging here, the energy that enables us to merge, is pure empathy, pure compassion. Awareness, consciousness of another's feelings, is the core skill that enables a soul to merge skillfully, fully, and considerately.*

But souls on this plane also have to know how to disengage. We have to know how to flow back out of one another. Exercises that lead to increased skill in this area are also built in to the earthly relationship process.

What is this merging like—on your plane? Dare I ask this? Is it pleasurable, like sex?

[Laughter.] *Why are you so squeamish about this?*

It just seems so odd. Talking to a messenger about sex. It seems somewhat sacrilegious to me and rather bizarre.

[More laughter.] *And this from a doctor. Yes, our merging is pleasurable but it is not like sex, at least the garden variety of sex most human beings experience. I guess the best way to put this is that our merging is pure and indescribably higher. Earthly sex is only a pale shadow of the joy emancipated souls feel when they interact with each other at the highest level here.*

How do these "exercises" work? What is the basic strategy behind them?

We recommend that most humans set it up so that they have a few peak experiences early on to remind them of what the whole thing is all about, to remind them of where they are going. In these experiences, all of the components—the body, the heart, various subtle emotional currents, and the spirit are merged simultaneously. The experiences of young lovers and newlyweds are good examples.

Once this phase has been completed, the real work begins. After they have been reminded of the final goal, the final point of evolution they are trying to achieve, earthly souls then go about the business of working on specific deficiencies. Some of these exercises involve considerable pain, but they are very helpful in the long run.

One way of looking at this is that they first go to the top of the mountain, where they can see the final destination from on high. Then they descend back into the forest, where they must do a great deal of difficult work to get to the promised land. Sometimes the courses that must be mastered in this phase are unpleasant.

[*Pause.*] You mean like having a broken heart?

That's one good example, yes. Souls that wish to expand their capacity to love at the heart level typically set their lives up so that their heart will be broken in one or more ways. Obviously, we counsel them extensively in this area. Locking the self into a course of heartbreak will involve enormous pain. We make sure everyone is clearly aware of this. But heartbreak is superb for expanding compassion and empathy, and most souls elect to undergo it in spite of the suffering involved.

[*Silence.*] Let me ask you this: What about people who don't have anybody, people who are looking for a relationship, a soul mate, but can't find one?

What is your question exactly? You'll have to be more specific.

[Pause.] I know people who are very worthy and very loving who cannot seem to find a good relationship no matter what they do. What I want to know is why can't they find a relationship? What is wrong in this situation?

What makes you think anything is wrong? Who are you to say that someone else's life is unfolding "incorrectly"? I'm telling you, it's all perfect. Being alone and searching for love can teach a person many valuable things. Some people set their lives up intentionally so that they will undergo periods of solitude.

But this is not always the case?

No. Some souls leave things open. They elect not to lock themselves into a course of solitude and can then change things if they want to.

So these people actually have a chance of finding someone? [Pause.] Can messengers help people who are alone find a suitable soul mate?

[Laughing.] *Of course.*

How do you do it? How do you go about helping someone find their perfect companion? If someone is alone and starts praying for divine help, messengeric help, what exactly do you do to help them? What is the process like? I'm fascinated.

Well, first of all, you have to keep in mind that "we" don't "do" anything, per se. At the deepest level a human being's will or intent is our intent, and our intent is the same as God's intent. I can't say this enough: Don't get confused about this issue. We are all the same being with the same goal. None of us "do" anything to anyone else.

Only when you understand this can you understand the process of divine assistance. Do you remember that we told you we are your thoughts, we are your prayers?

I remember.

Good. When a person prays to find a soul mate, their prayers radiate from their soul. Their faith becomes an energizing force that triggers a chain of events. [Pause.] We become their prayers. We carry the message, the force of their prayers into the Divine mind where everything is known. In this field of infinite knowledge and infinite love, we find a suitable match. When the match has been found, we analyze the person's current situation so that we understand every nuance of the chains of cause and effect that intersect their lives. This information is easily obtained through Infinite Intelligence, which knows everything.

Once this phase has been completed—actually the word "phase" is misleading because this happens instantaneously within the divine mind—certain things become very clear. We can easily see how to bring the two beings together.

How do you then go about this?

Following the prime directive, we are very subtle in our interventions. We choose a course of action that will involve the slightest possible disruption of the material plane. For example, we might appear as an interesting cloud in a sunset that makes one of the involved individuals pause for a moment to admire the beauty of the sky. That pause resets the timing of the person's life very slightly. But this tiny change leads to another change and another and another until the effect grows into a major change a month or a year later. Ultimately, the two individuals cross paths and are brought together very nicely. Whenever this happens, the two individuals feel quite rightly that it was somehow their "fate" or "destiny" to meet. What they don't know is their fates weren't externally foisted upon them. People design their own destinies.

[Pause.] Would I be right in thinking that the way the person prays to solicit your help is fairly critical?

Absolutely. The whole process is an extension of the original prayer. If the prayer is flawed, the process is flawed and nothing will happen.

What is the correct way to pray?

You know that. Everybody should know that. It's all over the New Testament and other holy books. There is nothing complicated or secret about the correct *way to pray—about finding a soul mate or solving any other problem. You tell me: What does the Bible say?*

[*Pause.*] Are you referring to the part that says we are to pray "believing"?

[*Laughing.*] *This isn't so difficult, is it? When a person prays believing, it means he or she is seeing the result as if it had already come to pass. When a person visualizes the end result clearly and with unwavering conviction—as if it were already a part of their reality—our job is effortless and automatic. At that point, we become the person's positive thoughts. That is our nature, the divine nature. We are the garden. As a manifestation of God, the infinite society of angelic beings is an incredibly fertile soil, a field of infinite possibilities that germinates seeds with unerring accuracy.*

But this process of altering our chains of cause and effect— I would assume it takes time.

Chain reactions of cause and effect normally involve the passage of what you call "time." In fact, you could accurately define "time" as "the process by which cause and effect unfolds." As you were told, there is almost always a delay between the sowing of the thought seed and its germination into a fruit-bearing tree. You also know why your world has been set up with a delay process. The delay protects you from injuring yourselves excessively. It gives you time to correct impulsive and illogical thought forms.

The mechanism of the delay has to do with the cause and effect process and with our need to remain subtle and transparent when we alter the cause and effect process. I need to make clear, however, that soul mates are rarely brought together in the way I have just described.

What is the usual way?

Soul mates bring themselves together—in advance. In almost all cases, soul mates already know each other, before their lives on Earth. Before they take birth, they set things up so that they will meet at just the right time to accomplish specific goals they feel are important.

Like what? What kinds of goals are you talking about?

One of the most common goals is a deepening of the bond that already exists between them. Two souls that are already bonded often wish to grow yet closer, as is the case with your friend who just died and his wife. Such individuals design their lives so that this will be accomplished in a very definitive and efficient manner.

Actually, one of the best ways to grow closer is through separation. The feeling of separation makes soul mates appreciate each other all the more when they finally "find" each other. As you often say there, "absence makes the heart grow fonder." This is what happened with you and your own wife.

So we *did* know each other?

[Laughter.] *That would be putting it mildly.*

So that's why I didn't meet her until I was in my thirties? That's why I went through such a long period of failed relationships and extended solitude?

You tell me. How did it work?

If that's what happened, then I will have to admit it worked incredibly well. By the time I met her I was in a position to really appreciate her. [*Pause.*] So that's why we are so close and why the relationship has been so successful?

What can I say?

[*Silence.*] There's something else I've been puzzling over.

Why is it that when two people are really in love and deeply committed to each other for their entire lives, their bodies deteriorate and their physical passion wanes in old age? That doesn't seem fair at all. It seems to me that if things were really fair, a devoted couple would be rewarded with increased physical attraction as their years of faithful commitment lengthen.

[Laughing.] *That's a very shortsighted view of things. If physical attraction increased as a couple aged, it would harm them immeasurably. Keep* in mind that both parties are headed for a plane in which they will have no physical bodies. What they really want to accomplish is to increase their ability to remain bonded and committed without bodies. The whole thing is about learning to merge perfectly at the level of Spirit. This is one of the endpoints of evolution.

They want to practice for the state that lies ahead. What better way to do this than to remain together as their bodies slowly fall apart. The learning process is heightened when one person passes away before another. [Laughing.] It's not "unfair" in the least. The system is quite perfect and works beautifully.

You said "at least for a while." What did you mean by that? That after a period on the angelic plane they will eventually take birth again as human beings and have another relationship?

Not exactly. I keep telling you—it's just not that simple. [Pause.] After a period of existence on this plane—here where I am—the couple may elect to enter another level of being. But there are many, many dimensions—many, many worlds other than your own. They may choose to pass through a plane that is totally different from anything in your universe and offers completely new lessons. Those dimensions and the worlds and beings within them are beyond description. There are no human words or concepts that could possibly describe them.

Would it be safe to say, however, that two soul mates will always choose to stay together with each other?

Yes and no. Soul mates by definition will nearly always remain bonded for eternity. But there may be more than two soul mates in a group. Soul mates may consist of extended families, and members may assume many different roles with each other in new existences.

How many soul mates may be in one of these groups?

Typically a group with anywhere from three or four to, say, several hundred will form the core or nucleus of the soul mate group. But the extended soul mate group may contain billions, as is the case with the souls on Earth.

Are you saying that all of the people on Earth are actually soul mates?

Basically, yes. In fact, all of the fifty trillion cells in your bodies are soul mates. All of the molecules of water in the ocean are soul mates. All of the molecules of gas within a star are soul mates, and all the stars in a galaxy are soul mates. It's all so much bigger than you humans can imagine. You are so terribly anthropomorphic that you can't conceive of any form of intelligence other than human intelligence. Very silly, really. If you only knew.

As far as the souls on Earth are concerned, in reality most of you know one another and are terribly fond of one another. You have set up an amazingly elaborate system of interwoven relationships that you designed to help you correct certain problems you have experienced in getting together. It is working very well, I might add.

I especially like the developments in communication and transportation that you have thrown in. The Internet is especially promising. A very nice touch. Before long you will all be able to share information with each other and visit each other with great fluidity. That will help enormously. But remember, you are on a plane that uses processes of cause and effect to keep things moving. So this won't happen overnight. It will all take time.

So we aren't going to blow each other up? There isn't going to be a gigantic Armageddon like some people say? I've never bought into that anyway.

[Great laughter.] Of course not. That's nonsense. The Armageddon, the Rapture, all of that will happen, all right, but you have to realize that they will happen inside you. These are metaphors for things that happen to the soul as it passes through critical phases of evolution.

Chapter Eight

John was an extraordinarily intelligent person, a genius in his own right. A brilliant attorney, he had specialized in medical malpractice and was one of the most successful litigators in his state. I hadn't seen him in several years. I knew that he was sick—his daughter had written to me describing his condition—but nothing could have prepared me for what I was seeing.

He was dying in a most agonizing way. Parkinson's disease, one of the most aggressive cases his physicians had ever seen, had paralyzed him completely. His once powerful frame was ravaged, reduced to the specter of a gaunt scarecrow. His hands were clutched to his chest in tight fists. Every muscle in his body was constricted in a rigid spasm. Even his eyelids were affected, and he was able to open and close them only with incredible effort.

But the real nightmare was that his mind was still functioning intact. Parkinson's doesn't destroy the intellect, only the body. Although it was too horrible to contemplate, the truth slowly dawned on me. He was still in there, still thinking away a mile a minute with that amazing intellect—a vigorous and penetrating mind cut off from humanity forever.

.I knew what John was doing, though. He was meditating. He had always loved to meditate and had become an expert during his lifetime. Now he had nothing else to do.

Although he couldn't say a word, I thought I knew what he was thinking that moment as I looked down at him. Although his tongue was totally paralyzed I felt that he was pleading with me, screaming at me, "Do something! For God's sake, you of all people should know better! We don't need words. Talk to me. Listen to me! It's all at the level of Spirit now."

I said nothing about this to his daughter, who had accompanied me to the nursing home. It was far too strange a thing to admit openly, but I was going to try to talk to him. I knew that it was possible to speak with newly departed souls and to messengers—that it wasn't difficult at all. And I knew from previous conversations that people don't necessarily die all at once. It was possible, I reasoned, that John was partially in the next world and that he could communicate from that realm as a newly awakening spirit.

Are you there?

Oh, I'm here all right.

It's horrible—your condition, I mean. I can't believe what has happened to you.

What are you talking about?

The Parkinson's, the paralysis.

Oh, that. I've practically forgotten about that.

So it's true, you really are halfway over to the other side?

No, I'd say I'm all the way over.

But your body, it's still lying there, it's…

[Laughter.] *It's perfect! Did you ever read that Jack London book* The Star Rover?

Yes, when I was a kid.

Well, it was all true. Do you remember that book?

I believe it was based on a true story. I recall that it was about a prisoner who was tortured in solitary confinement for many years. They put him in a full-length straightjacket until he could barely breathe and left him like that for weeks on end.

Right, and do you remember what happened?

The claustrophobia and the immobilization were so horrible, so unbearable, that he left his body and traveled to many places, even to different worlds and other stars.

Exactly. It works great.

So that's what has happened to you?

Nice setup, wouldn't you say? I think I did a pretty nice job all in all.

Are you out of your mind? You knowingly consented to this?

[Laughter.] *Before I was born, we all talked about it and, knowing what I knew, I decided this would be the perfect ending for me. To be locked in total paralysis with nothing left to do but meditate.*

What is it like, to be there on that plane?

The best way I can describe it is to say that it is perfectly fluid. There is no resistance. You think a thought and it's...right there, right in front of you. You think of being somewhere and you're instantly there. The speed of light is not the speed limit of the universe: Thought travels instantaneously.

Are you an "angel" then?

That's not how I would describe myself, no. We don't really use that word. The word "angel" is loaded with all sorts of distorted anthropomorphic connotations. But I guess that's what I am, what we are here.

I really want to ask you something.

Go ahead.

Have you seen God?

[Laughter.] *Everybody has seen God.*

What does he look like?

Everything and nothing, all at once.

Does God have a kind of body?

The universe is God's body. You know that. It's obvious.

I know this at one level, but at another level I can't see it at all. The universe is so spread out. The stars, the galaxies are separated by hundreds, thousands of light-years. How is that a body? Nothing is connected.

Nonsense. It's all connected together perfectly, and it all thinks, just like a gigantic brain.

I don't see how that is possible. The universe isn't at all like a brain. A brain is made up of billions of cells that are all connected together with an intricate web of synapses.

And how does this brain work? At the most basic level, how does a brain, or a computer, for that matter, "think"?

[*Pause.*] I guess you could say that it is a series of on/off switches. A computer has a vast number of tiny switches that register either a one or a zero. A synapse in a brain works the same way. Neurotransmitters travel from one brain cell to another. When they reach the other brain cell they lock into a receptor. That turns the receptor, which acts as a switch, on. So the receptor receives a tiny bit of information. It is either on or off, either a one or a zero. You hook a few billion of these together and you have a huge amount of computing or thinking power. That is how intelligence is formed.

That is how the universe is hooked up too.

But that doesn't make any sense. Like I said, it's all spread out over thousands of light-years. How can you say it is hooked up like a brain?

[*Laughter.*] *From the viewpoint of that little molecule of neurotransmitter, two neurons are many miles from each other too. The scale is just different, so you can't see it.*

But there are no neurotransmitters that travel from one star to another. There is nothing to hook them together, nothing to convey information from one to another. They are completely disconnected.

That is totally inaccurate. Have you ever seen the stars?

Go on.

How do you see a star?

What do you mean?

What is the physiological mechanism that enables you to see a star?

Light waves travel through space from the star to my eyes. They collide with molecules on the retina where chemical reactions trigger little on/off switches that send sensory impulses to the brain.

Are the light waves from the star interpreted as "information" by your brain?

Yes.

Waves can carry vast amounts of information. A single electromagnetic wave can transmit an entire television documentary or a symphony to you. [Laughter.] There is a lot more going on between stars than you realize. Think about it: What else passes between stars?

Well, I guess if you want to be complete you would have to include all the rest of the electromagnetic spectrum—radio waves, gamma rays, X-rays—that sort of thing.

Anything else?

[Pause.] Gravitational waves? Gravity travels in waves, doesn't it?

And you think a simple little bundle of neurotransmitters traveling between two neurons carries a lot of information, eh? That's the trouble with human beings, at least while you are on Earth in your little bodies: You think you are the be-all and end-all. [Laughter.] You even thought the Earth was the center of the whole universe for a few thousand years! You haven't really advanced that far, in spite of what you think.

Man was created in God's image, not vice versa. Here I am trying to convince you that God's brain might be just as good as a human being's brain, while the truth is that your brain is but a tiny replica of the universal mind.

A human being has about ten billion brain cells, and several trillion synapses connect them together. This number is sufficient to support consciousness—even self-consciousness and God consciousness. Imagine what would happen if you hooked up a billion, billion, billion brain cells with a trillion, trillion, trillion synapses between them. There are billions of galaxies, and each contains billions of stars. Can you begin to understand? Can you imagine what such a mind could think or do?

I can't even conceive of that.

That is the most intelligent thing you have said.

I am still having trouble with this, though. In a human brain, cells can grow and change. Synapses become easier to use the more they are used. The ability to shift and change at the cellular level gives us the ability to remember and learn. The stars don't change in response to one another. The "synapses" between them don't "remember." How can learning and real consciousness take place in the universal brain you are describing?

There you go again. How do you know what information really passes between one star and another? Who says they don't change in response to one another? Of course they change in response to the information they receive. For example, what happens when one star approaches another?

Well, I would have to admit that their gravitational fields affect one another. They move slightly toward one another as gravity waves are "exchanged."

Every star in the universe sends out gravity waves and affects every other star in a very real, very physical way. The effect close stars have on one another is strong. The effect distant stars have on one another is very slight, but it is still present. The same goes for all the other kinds of wave-forms that pass from one star to the next.

Electromagnetic waves, X-rays, radio waves, gamma rays—all of these have an effect on the other stars they fall upon. If two stars are very close to each other, they cause profound changes in each other. They each affect each other's magnetic fields, internal flows of gases, chemical compositions, trajectories, even each other's ultimate life spans.

I can see this, but I can also see another flaw in your theory.

[Great laughter.] *Oh, according to you this is "theory," eh?*

I'm sorry. I can't see with your perspective, so it is still just theory to me. The other problem I see is the way you are comparing stars to brain cells. The analogy seems to fall apart there. Stars aren't cells. Brain cells are structures that are highly organized at the molecular level. Stars, on the other hand, are nothing but gigantic balls of randomly circulating gas. It doesn't matter what they transmit to each other. They aren't alive in the first place, any more than a rock is alive.

Oh, stars are alive, all right. So are rocks. You just have to shift gears for a minute to see how. Let's start with a rock. What is a rock exactly?

It is a lump of molecules.

Really? And what is a molecule?

A bunch of atoms that are bound together.

How are they bound together? How are any two atoms bound together?

Two atoms bind together when they come very close together and actually begin sharing electrons.

What does that mean, "sharing electrons"?

It means that one electron orbits both atoms. It spins around one atom, then zooms over and spins around the other for a while. Then it goes back to the first one again.

Do electrons carry any information?

Of course not. They are tiny, lifeless bits of energy.

Oh, really? How are they any different from a molecule of neurotransmitter? According to your view of things, a molecule of neurotransmitter is also a tiny, lifeless object. Yet you already said that it carries information from one brain cell to another. Think about it.

I guess you could make a case that electrons carry "information" in the sense that they can spin different ways, occupy different orbits around atoms, and can have different amounts of energy.

That is information pure and simple. Electrons carry information from one atom to another when they are bound together in an electron. Now, take this one step further. What happens to electrons in a metal?

Their orbits aren't limited to two atoms. Electrons flow in and around and through all the atoms in a metallic substance. That's why electricity, which is a flow of electrons, can move through a metal wire many miles in length.

So you would agree that all the atoms in a metallic object or a crystal are connected?

Yes.

Then don't they all share information via the flow of electrons?

In a sense, I suppose so.

How many atoms are in a small crystal or a small rock?

Trillions upon trillions upon trillions.

So you agree that a small rock has many more atoms than a human brain has cells?

I suppose so.

And they are all sharing information?

Yes. But atoms aren't cells. Atoms aren't alive. It doesn't matter what "information" they share.

How do you know atoms aren't alive?

It's obvious. Atoms are simple nuclei surrounded by electrons. How could they be alive?

It's not obvious. What's in the nucleus of an atom?

Not much. Protons and neutrons, which are in turn composed of a small collection of subatomic particles like quarks and leptons.

[Laughter.] *That's it? That's all, eh? Just a "small collection of subatomic particles."* [Great peals of laughter.]

What's so funny?

You are. All of you. [Lengthy laughter.]

Would you mind letting me in on the joke?

It's just funny, looking back. I was there too. Throughout history humans have assumed that what they can see with their eyes and instruments is all there is. Very silly, really, and a bit dumb. [Pause.] *Do you believe in infinity?*

I guess so.

Do you think God is infinite?

I don't know for sure. But I think it is likely.

You think it is possible that God, the Universe, is infinite but that atomic nuclei are just a small collection of subatomic particles?

Most likely, yes. What are you getting at?

What are subatomic particles made out of? What's inside a lepton or a quark?

No one knows for sure.

No one knows, but you automatically assume that they are somehow the be-all and end-all, right?

Are you trying to say that subatomic particles are made of still smaller subatomic particles—sub-subatomic particles and on and on into infinity?

[Laughter.] *If you only knew. What if I were to tell you that the average "quark" you speak of contains many sub-subatomic particles, and each one of those contains many sub-sub-subatomic particles?*

I wouldn't know what to think. It boggles the mind. I can't quite conceive of that.

Nonsense, of course you can. [Laughter.] *So where do you think it all ends? Do you think there is some tiny little particle that is the end of it all?*

Somehow I hope so. It is hard to conceive of a universe that just keeps going and going, down and down, into smaller and smaller pieces forever.

So? So what if you can't conceive of it? What difference does that make?

Are you saying that's how things really are?

Maybe. Maybe not. [Laughter.] *I wouldn't want to spoil things for you. Besides, you wouldn't believe me if I told you anyway. Neither would you believe me if I told you that the infinitely small merges seamlessly with the infinitely large and that the impossible thing that connects them is, in fact, "God."* [More laughter.] *But let's get back to the rock. You said that atoms are not alive. That they couldn't be alive because they are "just nuclei with a few electrons orbiting them." Will you admit now that you have no solid evidence to back this up? That your "knowing" they are not alive is really just an assumption. Will you admit that you really have no idea at all whether they are alive or not?*

I guess so. I guess that it is possible they are alive. Actually, I have always thought intuitively that they are alive in some way. I just couldn't see how, that's all. I couldn't visualize a mechanism through which they could be alive.

Well, if a small rock has enough machinery inside to support a kind of brain and a potential consciousness, then why can't a star be alive?

If you really wanted to reach, I guess you could make a kind of weird case that stars are somehow alive and "conscious."

[Loud laughter.] *A "weird case," huh? According to this one tiny condescending human being, it might just be possible that stars are alive! Well, that is very big of you to admit.* [More laughter.]

You don't have to mock me.

I'm not mocking you. It's just that when you get over here and see how things really work, it'll knock your socks off! You're going to love it. The fact is that it is all hooked up together. Everything in the whole universe is connected together by an infinite web of synapses. It's all thinking, all feeling, all creating, all at once.

Why does it look so inanimate, then? Why haven't our scientists been able to figure this out?

That's easy. Imagine you are a brain cell for a minute. What does the brain around you look like? If you were a brain cell, would you even know that you were part of a brain? Would there be any way you could know that the brain you were in was thinking? Of course not! You wouldn't have the vaguest idea that you were really part of a gigantic thinking machine. You would be stuck down in some deep, dark part of the brain, barely aware that there were a few other cells nearby. You would assume that you were the center of the universe and that the cells adjacent to you were the entire remainder of the universe. All the while the brain around you could be composing a symphony, thinking about God, or even reaching enlightenment, and you would never know it.

[*Pause.*] Is our society a kind of brain? Is it alive and conscious like a living organism, like a kind of brain?

Few of you know it yet, but your human society is an organism that is very much alive and conscious. Figure it out. What are the "neurons" in this "brain"?

People? We have nearly six billion of them. That seems like plenty of "neurons" for a brain.

Good. And what are the neurotransmitters that allow people to share information?

Words? Books? Television? The Internet?

Excellent. Plus the viruses and bacteria that pass among you, the visual stimuli or light waves that you share, your music—all of these things connect you and allow you to share information.

What is this brain doing? Where is it going? What is it thinking about?

Survival. Achieving harmony and peace of mind. As is the case with all liv-ing organisms, it thinks about what it will create. It dreams and plans and wants to make a better world for itself—all the usual things sentient entities spend their time with.

[*Silence.*] A few minutes ago you mentioned enlightenment. What is that? What is enlightenment?

It is the realization that you are not the individual, not the neuron, but the whole. That you are actually the universal mind. You know. You touched enlightenment once for a few days. Lots of people have.

When?

You know.

[*Pause.*] You mean that one time in the cornfield?

Yes. Think back for a minute. Remember how that happened?

It was in my Zen phase in my early twenties. I had been meditat-ing for months, trying to do this Zen koan—you know—a question that has no rational answer. I was working on the koan "What is the sound of one hand clapping?" I went out into a field and started meditating on this question harder than I ever had before. I made up my mind not to get up until I figured it out. I was quite an extremist at that point in my life. Very intense.

I had been doing this for about five hours without standing up when I finally just gave up in exhaustion. I just stopped thinking, about anything. I sat this way for a while, I don't know how long. I lost track of time when I suddenly felt like…like the bottom of my mind fell out. That is the only way I can describe it. Like I was a small bucket and the bottom of the bucket just broke apart and I kind of spilled out into all the rest of the ocean. That there was no "me" anymore.

Suddenly the answer was obvious. It had been there right before me the whole time. I clapped both hands together wildly and laughed until I was sick. I knew that I didn't really have two hands. I saw that there is only one hand, one single, unified thing in all the universe.

Do you remember what that felt like, what the world around you looked like from that perspective?

Vaguely. That was a long time ago. It was like everything was alive, humming and whirring like a gigantic beehive. Every rock, every plant, every cloud in the sky, every molecule, everything was buzzing, swimming with life, and radiating a luminous transparent light. It felt like it was all light, all love, and yet all…a gigantic hilarious joke or something. I just laughed and laughed and laughed.

What you were experiencing were the thoughts of the whole world around you, the thoughts of the greater mind of which you are a tiny part. That was a tiny taste of enlightenment—another evolutionary endpoint—when it becomes permanent.

I hardly consider myself enlightened. In fact, I'm somewhat of an idiot.

Oh, don't misunderstand me. You are far from enlightened. You slipped back into the delusional state you are presently in long ago. Now you're just a doofus like everybody else. That was simply a little taste you were given to keep you going. To let you know where you are supposed to go, where you will eventually end up. Actually, you're doing reasonably well, all in all.

[*Silence.*] Something else.

Yes?

How big is the universe, really? Is this universe all there is?

You said you believed in the possibility of infinity, that God might conceivably be infinite, right?

It's possible, yes.

What if I were to tell you that the thing you call the universe, the expanse of galaxies that stretches as far as your most powerful telescopes can see, is but a tiny particle within the greater whole?

It would almost make me sick. That notion staggers the imagination.

Imagine for a minute that you are a tiny creature in a single atom in a small rock at the top of a mountain in a vast panorama of mountains. Imagine that you discover after great effort and many years that the atom you thought was your entire universe is actually surrounded by other atoms, other complete universes.

Then you discover that there are trillions upon trillions of these universes all held together, all functioning together as a conscious entity in a mass called a rock.

Now imagine that you discover that this rock is surrounded by trillions of other rocks that form an enormous mountain, and that this mountain is surrounded by hundreds of other...

Stop already. This is out of control!

[Laughter.] *This thing you call your universe is an incredibly tiny part of the real universe. The real universe is so vast that even your greatest scientists, your greatest thinkers could never conceive of it. None of them can ever fathom its depth, its complexity. And certainly none of them can ever comprehend its intelligence. Infinite Intelligence is to you as your greatest genius is to a worm—only a trillion times more.*

I never saw John again. Three days after this conversation was recorded, he died silently in his bed at the nursing home.

Chapter Nine

The ambulance alerted us over the radio that they were bring-
ing in a suicide victim. They didn't know if he was still alive
but were doing everything they could to save him. When he came
through the door and we got him up on the gurney in the trauma
room, however, I could see he was a goner.

The twenty-two-year-old had been thrown in jail on rape charges
the night before. While doing his routine rounds, the jailer had
found him hanging by a braided sheet from a water pipe.

We spent about fifteen minutes trying to revive him with the
usual aggressive measures, but there was no hope. I pronounced
him dead, arranged to have his estranged family notified back East,
and retired sadly to the call room.

I didn't mean it. Get me down from here. Stop this right now.
Easy, guy. Nice and slow. Just pretend you're lying down for a nap.
Who the hell are you? Get out of here if you know what's good for you.
You're fighting it. Just relax back. No one will bother you. You are going
back home.

I'm dead, aren't I? That's what this is all about, isn't it? Leave me alone. I'm going to hell, God damn you. Leave me the hell alone!

There is no hell. But you can thrash around here confused and angry for as long as you want. That's the closest thing to hell we have for you.

I want to go to hell.

Nonsense.

I am in hell. Jesus, look at that. Here they come. It's them. [Screaming.] *They're going to take me away.*

Nonsense. You're making them. Stop looking at them. Look over this way. Do you see that figure? Look at the light. Just keep looking at the bright area over there.

[Pause.] *Who are you? You're different. What do you want? I know you, don't I? Go away.*

Want to see something?

Leave me alone!

Look.

[Silence, then weeping.] *I didn't mean it. I was drunk.*

I know. Come over this way. That's better.

[Crying.] *Are they gone? You mean I don't have to go there?*

I've got a better idea. See that bright stuff? Come on. Let's check it out. Don't try to move. Here, I'll pull you through like this.

[Silence.] Is it over?

Yes. Everything's okay now. Do you want to talk?

There are so many things I want to know about. My head is swimming with questions. I don't even know where to begin.

Do you feel that it is important to ask your questions in a certain order? Why should that matter?

Okay. I'll just dive on in: What happens to people on Earth when they die? Do we all become messengers?

One thing is for sure. You don't simply cease to exist. You, the real you, what you call your "soul" is far too valuable to be so senselessly wasted. The great Creator, like all the great creative people who have lived on Earth, abhors waste.

The intelligence that brought the universe into being and keeps it moving is a consummate recycler and conservator of energy and resources. The accomplishments of the soul are the treasures that you have laid up in heaven. These are the valuables you take with you into the next world to use in your new work.

To answer the second part of your question, yes, most of you become what you call messengers when your bodies cease to function and you pass into this realm. You can think of yourselves as messengers in training.

[Silence.] Are there different kinds of angels? Are we training to be different kinds of angels?

Although you are all training to be angels, you are not all training to become the same kind of angel. An engineer on Earth might be training to become an angel that helps design and construct some aspect of the physical plane after passing on. A musician might be preparing to harmonize certain kinds of energy fields in the next realm. A farmer could be learning skills that will enable him to oversee certain processes in the plant kingdom after crossing over.

What about angels like you and the others that have spoken with me? I would assume some of us are training to be angels like you, angels that work directly with people.

Some of you are perfecting skills that will help you function as what you often refer to as "guardian angels" and in some cases as "evolution angels"—like me.

The "courses" that lead to expertise in this area—what are they like?

Parents, clergy, counselors and therapists, firemen, paramedics, police, caretakers, social workers, nurses, and physicians like yourself all have one thing in common: They wait to be called to solve serious human problems. The responsibilities and skills learned in these lines of work are essential for guardian angels. For evolution angels additional study is required. You're doing some work in this area yourself.

[Pause.] How many kinds of angels are there?

[Laughing.] *How many kinds of people are there?*

Okay. Let me ask you this: Is there really a hierarchy of angels like those described in medieval literature?

Not exactly. The concept of a hierarchy is inadequate to describe the way we are organized. "Hierarchy" is a human word and suggests that some members within a system are more important than others. How can I put this in a way you will understand?

[Pause.] *It is true that some of us are more powerful than others, but the idea that some of us are more important than others is entirely inaccurate. Do you remember when we told you that angels are like God's fingers?*

Yes.

To understand us, to understand God, keep reminding yourself that you have been created in the image of the Creator. Look at your arm. Some of its muscles are more powerful than the others, right?

That much is obvious, yes.

Would you say that the powerful muscles of your upper arm are more important than the delicate muscles of your thumb? Would you say your index finger is more important than your middle finger?

I would have to say no—they just have different functions.

The network of angels is like your system of muscles and tissues and organs. It has been arranged so that some of us have greater power and more responsibilities than others, but such angels are no more important than very small angels.

This is intriguing. What are the really big angels like? What do they do?

[Laughing.] *First of all, keep in mind the kind of scale we are working with. Remember, the universe is infinite. This means that it is infinitely large and infinitely small. It extends forever and forever in both directions. All of the stars, all of the galaxies in the entire system your earthly astronomers refer to as the "universe" are but a tiny particle in the whole. On the other hand, the smallest subatomic particles your physicists can detect are vast universes unto themselves. They contain an infinite number of universes within.*

With that in mind, let me say this: As far as Earth is concerned, some angels oversee and administer entire cities, even entire countries. Still others oversee entire galaxies and universes. But even these angels are little more than drops in the vast sea of angels. And they know it. So they waste no time thinking they are more important than angels that happen to be smaller than themselves.

What are the smallest angels like? [*Pause.*] Are you telling me that atoms and subatomic particles like quarks and leptons also have angels? That is a bizarre concept.

[Laughing.] *Of course.*

People here would think that concept quite ludicrous. It sounds like something a schizophrenic would hallucinate. Nobody will believe that.

[Great laughter.] *Should that surprise me? Humans thought the Earth was the center of the universe for centuries. When a few insightful individuals tried to show you otherwise, you laughed at them too—or worse. You haven't really come that far. You still think you are the center of the universe, that you are the only intelligent beings in the infinite world that surrounds your tiny realm.*

You have a long, long history of looking at the truth as though it were insane. Let people think what they want. The truth will ultimately be revealed.

By science, you mean?

By any method. All your disciplines and systems will end up at the same place if they look long enough and hard enough at the fabric of reality.

Well, let me ask this a little differently. If angels work at the atomic and subatomic level, will scientists eventually be able to detect them?

They have already detected them. They just can't explain them. [Laughing.] *They just can't accept what they are seeing. Are you familiar with the wave-particle dilemma?*

Sure. For decades now physicists have been dealing with an enigma that doesn't seem to make any sense. They can't tell if light is a wave or a particle. It can't possibly be both, and yet it appears that it is.

To make matters worse, when particle physicists *decide* to look for a wave they *find* a wave, but when they *decide* to look for a particle they *find* a particle. It drives them absolutely crazy. No matter how they slice it, it appears that the sheer intent or consciousness of the experimenter determines the way the particle behaves, the way it manifests. And yet this is utterly "impossible."

Their conscious intent really is influencing the behavior of the particles they are observing. Do you remember what happens when you pray? What did we say about that?

You said that our thoughts become angels, that angels serve as a kind of vehicle that transmits the power of our beliefs, our visualizations, and helps them shape reality.

So? Put it together yourself.

[*Pause.*] Are you saying that the thoughts of a physicist are taken up by "messengers" associated with the particles they are observing and that the angels then produce the changes that are observed? That sounds ridiculous—utterly delusional. I would be embarrassed to even mention this to someone else.

[Great laughter.] *The reason it sounds so strange has a lot to do with language problems inherent in our discussion. To begin with, there is a fundamental problem calling the conscious entities that work with atomic particles "messengers." In reality, it doesn't matter what you call them. Physicists call them "photons." You're calling them "messengers." If you want, you can make up a new name and call them "phogels."* [Laughter.] *Who cares what you call them? What difference does it make? They are what they are and they are conscious.*

Actually, Niels Bohr, the physicist who formulated the principles of quantum physics, said many years ago that he thought these particles were conscious.

As I told you, we are essentially light. The conscious entities "with" the photons and the photons themselves are not two different things. Angels aren't really "associated" with subatomic particles, we don't "administrate" them, and we don't "inhabit" them. We are the light. Don't get confused. It's very simple.

So all of the physicists that are now claiming that subatomic particles are somehow conscious are correct?

Of course. You know that.

Well, that's what I've thought for many years, but I just wanted to get it on record.

[Laughter.] *Oh, I'm sure that will settle it once and for all!*

You don't have to make fun of me.

[Softly.] *Now you know perfectly well I'm not making fun of you when we laugh. It's just that…how can I not laugh? That's just what we do. It's our nature, the nature of Spirit, to laugh and take things lightly.*

[*Pause.*] If light—if photons are actually conscious, do they have a kind of "personality"?

Of course.

That's nuts. And this personality is like…your personality—it laughs and takes things "lightly."

[More laughter.] *See? Talk about it long enough and your own words will lead you back to the truth!*

[*Long silence.*] Do you mind if I ask you some other things I have been wondering about?

Go ahead.

How many angels does a human being have? Do we only have one apiece?

That is like asking "How many angels can dance on the head of a pin?" It's the same as asking "How many ways can you see God manifested in the world around you?"

There is no limit to the number of angels a human can access. However, in most cases there is no need for a large number of angels. For the sake of clarity and simplicity, it is best to keep your relationship confined to one or, at most, several specific angels. In general, you will be able to have a more meaningful and consistent relationship with the angelic realm from your side if you confine your conscious contact to specific personalized entities.

Do people with high levels of earthly responsibility have very powerful angels? For example, what kinds of angels work with the president of a major nation?

Messengers possess varying degrees of authority, power, experience, and skill. You will attract or be assigned an angel that is appropriate for your own needs and skills. Understand, however, that needs and skills are rated much differently in the angelic realm than in your world.

In your world, position, intelligence, wealth, and authority are important criteria. However, these are minor criteria in our eyes; we think other things matter more. Messengers place great importance on a human being's efforts to relieve suffering and promote love and harmony. A human who gives generously and is actively engaged in activities that help others will be granted the most powerful of angels. This is one of the true meanings of the phrase "To him who has will be added more." If you have developed the inclination and the power to help others and exercise this power, more power will be added to you in the form of angelic assistance.

[Pause.] Here's something else I've been wondering about: Do angels frequent certain places? Do you prefer certain environments over others? If so, can human beings increase their chances of contact by being in such places?

No. We aren't attracted to places. We are attracted to certain states of consciousness. Many of you have glimpsed us while visiting physical environments classically associated with divine contact—mountaintops, deserts, isolated seascapes, and so forth. But the reason contact is somewhat more frequent in such places is because these places are conducive to a quiet, meditative, appreciative state of mind—not in us, but in the human beings perceiving us.

Are all angels "dead" in the sense that they have passed from this plane? Are there any angels that are alive in the conventional sense of the word?

Actually, there are many angels that are alive and on Earth. Many, many human beings function, at least part of the time, as angels. There is no law that says we can't enlist willing humans and put them to work in our projects. We do that with you and many of your colleagues periodically. And there is no law that says an angel, which is just another word for "agent of Spirit," cannot be alive in a body on Earth. Finally, there is no law that says humans cannot leave their bodies temporarily and function as pure Spirit.

This last thing you mentioned. How does that happen?

It happens all the time. It's very natural. As I said, Spirit is incredibly efficient. It uses every iota of energy and consciousness in the most effective way possible. There are many people who actually leave their bodies during the night and go to work for us on other planes. Once again, we have arranged for you and many people you know to do this from time to time. It's no big deal.

Is that what dreams are?

Certain dreams, yes. But most dreams are just dreams.

[*Silence.*] How do angels produce effects on the material plane? You said that you sometimes alter our chains of cause and effect in order to make certain changes here. But I don't understand how you would do this, how you could interface with and produce effects on the material plane if you have no physical form. I'm confused about that.

Remember the example you were given? A angel becomes a cloud in a sunset and a person stops for a moment to admire it. This pause results in a chain reaction of precisely calculated events. Do you remember that?

Yes.

That's how we do things. What I didn't mention, however, is that we rarely become a real, physical cloud. We could do that, certainly. An extension of God can do anything. We could become a physical cloud made of real water vapor and then quietly fade away. No one would notice anything peculiar. But, in general, we prefer more elegant solutions.

Because we are one with your thoughts and God's thoughts at the deepest level, we work most often at the level of subconscious thought. In this example, we could become the perception of a cloud—a mental image in the subject's mind. This image will have precisely the same effect as a physical cloud. Either way, the person we are working with will pause for a moment and her web of cause and effect will be suitably altered.

Is that what you do when you "materialize" as, say, a winged being surrounded by light?

[Laughter.] *Yes. Although we consider it a bit silly, sometimes we form an impression in a person's field of perception that mimics one of the classical stereotypes. Rarely, in carefully selected situations, we find it effective and permissible to appear in a way that matches a person's expectations. Most people expect us to appear with wings and so forth, so we give them what they want.*

[Chuckling.] So you don't have wings?

[Laughter.] *Does God have a long white beard and sit on a throne?*

Chapter Ten

It was a beautiful morning and Mr. Hanson was having a ball inspecting the woods behind one of his enormous wheat fields. It was hard to imagine how things could be any better. The fall air was crisp and clear. The golden leaves on the cottonwoods were rustling in a light wind. Most important, the elderly gentleman's two beloved sons walked with him, one on each side.

No one paid any attention to the log that lay before them on the deer path. The conversation was far too interesting. The three men went single file over it, the two sons going first in their eagerness. But Mr. Hanson was getting old. Perhaps it was his eyesight, perhaps it was the subtle awkwardness that comes with age that made him stumble as he crossed the fallen limb. Perhaps it was something else, something deep in the spirit, deep in himself.

He fell forward lightly, hit the ground with a soft thud, and fell silent.

"Dad? Dad, are you all right?" his elder son said, shaking his shoulder lightly.

Silence.

"Is he breathing?" the other asked, now anxious.

"My God, no. Run! Run as fast as you can and get an ambulance!" the eldest shouted as he turned his father over and started CPR. It took the ambulance almost an hour to get back to him. They had to carry him by foot through the woods nearly half a mile.

When he finally arrived at the ER, I didn't know what was wrong. His heart was barely beating. I assumed, as did the other physicians who came down for the Code Blue, that he had suffered a heart attack or perhaps a severe stroke—those were the only diagnoses that made any sense. While we kept him immobilized, he was intubated and then a cardiac pacer was placed through a vein into his heart. When we had his heart reasonably stabilized, a cross-table X-ray of his neck was taken as a formality. This is always done routinely when someone is brought into a trauma center with his neck immobilized.

Everyone gasped softly when the films were clipped to the bedside viewer: His neck was badly broken, the first cervical vertebra pushed back horribly over the second, causing a complete transection of his spinal cord—a freak occurrence in a minor fall. None of us had ever seen this happen from a simple stumble. No wonder he wasn't breathing. The nerves that supplied the diaphragm had been severed and his entire system had been thrown into shock.

He had no living will and his family was traumatized and bewildered. They wanted everything done. I called the helicopter, and he was flown to Denver within the hour. While we waited, I went back to the call room. He had already left his body. It was nothing more now than a mechanical shell waiting to expire. He was outside, there in the emergency room waiting silently for his trusted vehicle to fall away completely. He would officially die twelve hours later at the big hospital in the city.

As always, others were there on the other side to help him. As I waited for the helicopter, I began to write.

There are some things you've been wanting to ask but have been avoiding. Is this not so?

[*Tentatively.*] Yes, I guess you could say that.

Don't you think it's about time you broached the subject? You can't avoid this forever you know.

I would rather not get into this right now.

And why is that?

Because it's such a touchy subject, I suppose. I'm not sure I'm ready to hear the answers.

No. You're ready to hear them. You are already hearing them. You are just afraid to write them down. As usual, you are afraid of what others might think.

[*Pause.*] I don't want to upset anyone.

Even if knowing more of the truth would help them significantly along the path?

[*Long pause.*] Okay. Here goes: Who was Jesus?

[*Laughter.*] *Was that really so bad?*

I don't know. I haven't heard the answer yet.

Let me begin my answer with a question: What is your favorite picture of Jesus? What does it look like?

I don't have a favorite picture. I have never seen a single picture that depicts Jesus the way I see him in my mind's eye.

Oh, yes, you have. Think.

[*Pause.*] You mean that poster? The one that shows the fifty different faces of Jesus from fifty different cultures? The one that shows an American Jesus, a Chinese Jesus, an African Jesus, an American Indian Jesus, and so forth, all lined up together?

[Laughter. Then silence.]

Are you saying that's what Jesus looks like?

I didn't say anything, did I?

No, no, no...I think I understand what you're getting at, but I am asking a different question. I want to know what the *real* Jesus looked like, the one that walked the Earth two thousand years ago.

What difference does it make what he looked like? Besides, you have no idea what "real" is.

You know what I mean. I'm not referring merely to his physical appearance but to his overall presence. Was the historical Jesus, the one presented in the Gospels, like the real Jesus?

[*Silence.*] *Our code requires that we lead you through this particular question in such a way that you answer it yourself. The best way to begin is with the parable of the mustard seed. Do you remember that parable?*

Only roughly.

Then look it up.

[*Long pause.*] It says:

Another parable put he forth to them, saying, "The kingdom of heaven is like to a grain of mustard seed, which a man took, and sowed in his field: Which indeed is the least of all seeds; but when it is grown, it is the greatest among herbs, and becometh a tree, so that the birds of the air come and lodge in the branches thereof." (Matthew 13:31–32, KJV)

What do you think the mustard seed stands for in this parable?

It says right up front that it refers to "the kingdom of heaven."

Now, you know Jesus better than that. His parables always had several levels of meaning. What else could the seed represent?

[*Pause.*] Are you saying it represents Jesus himself?

Excellent. Now, knowing this, what does the parable tell you about Jesus?

I'm not exactly sure what you're getting at.

Simple. It means that Jesus was like a seed, an especially small seed, in fact.

A tiny baby born into abject poverty in a barn in the middle of the night. From this seed an enormous tree grew. Do you see the tree?

All the people that have come to believe in him? The churches of the world? The so-called Body of Christ?

Is that too big a stretch? Jesus was the son of man, the son of humanity. He looked like everyone's son because he was everyone's son.

But what the actual man was like when he walked the Earth is of relatively little importance. It's like looking at a gigantic towering redwood tree and obsessing over what the seed looked like. It's a bit silly. What difference does it make what the seed was like? The tree is all that matters now.

It seems to me that it matters because we could clarify many misconceptions and false beliefs about Christ if we could once and for all know the truth about his real nature.

[Laughter.] Surely you realize how naive that sounds? Everybody knows that churches and sects will fight and argue and judge one another and feel superior to one another no matter who says what. [More laughter.]

Come on. You've got to help me out on this. I don't know how you want me to pose this question. I am asking you very directly: What is the true nature of Christ? What was he really all about?

[Pause.] What really happened was like this: God wanted to insert a very potent element of knowledge and love into the world. With infinite intelligence he studied every aspect of your world in order to understand every conceivable chain of cause and effect. Do you remember what we told you about the way we work, how angels work when we want to alter the plane of cause and effect where you live?

You said that you make every effort to disrupt this plane in the most subtle way possible. That you try to figure out where you can make the slightest change that will inevitably produce the desired result through the process of cause and effect.

Right. Angels are facets of God, agents of God, and we go about our business in much the same way that God does. So you can learn a great deal about how God works by understanding our methods and techniques. Jesus was the smallest, most subtle change God could make in your world in order to bring about the desired result—the catalyst for a chain reaction leading to a huge billowing explosion of light and love and understanding—a chain reaction that is still gaining force two thousand years later. The man called Jesus was the tiny mustard seed that would blossom into the most enormous tree the world has ever known.

The truth is that Spirit planned every single, solitary aspect of the tree that has resulted while simultaneously respecting human free will and allowing it to express itself unfettered. Every branch, every leaf, and every cell was all foreseen. Every belief, every sect, and every church that is allied with the body of Christ is just as it should be. None is better than another. Each has a specific purpose and fulfills a specific need that keeps the whole alive and growing.

There are many, many kinds of people in many stages of personal evolution. For some, a fundamentalist approach is appropriate and correct. For others, a highly intellectual approach is appropriate and correct. For still others, such as yourself, a purely mystical approach with direct contact is appropriate and correct.

Christ looks like the poster with the fifty different faces. He was a tiny seed that was planted in the world in such a way that his memories would be perfect images of truth to every man and every woman who turned to him for inspiration.

[Pause.] So there really was an actual man named Jesus?

Does the tree exist?

Yes.

Then you tell me: Was there a seed or not?

[Pause.] Okay, if I grant you that it matters little in the cosmic scheme of things, do you mind if I still ask you what the original man was like, what the seed of the tree was like in real life?

No. I don't mind. But keep in mind that history is all in the past, all in the mind. Keep your eye on the present moment where you are right now. Concentrate on your function within the tree—on your duty to become a living legacy of love and tolerance and charity. That's all that should really matter to you or any Christian. The history is nothing but a diversion from these truly important pursuits.

[Pause.] Jesus was not a very imposing or physically impressive person during most of his life. This was intentional. Spirit wanted to make clear that wealth, power, physical beauty, and size were not important.

Jesus was small of stature. He was a Jew, from the Middle East, and had a very dark complexion even for a person of that region. He would undoubtedly be classified as "black" by contemporary, middle-class Americans. In spite of his ordinary countenance, he was nonetheless physically strong and very agile. He was, in truth, a carpenter—what you would call a blue-collar laborer—and worked with his hands. He was very good at what he did, extraordinarily artful. You should have seen the work he did. Precise and very beautiful.

He was highly intelligent, a genius of the highest magnitude, but few people could discern this. His mannerisms, his accent, and the way he often phrased things was very plain, very lower middle class—to put it in your terms. If you were to bump into him on the street, you would never recognize him as an enlightened being. [Laughter.] In fact, you do bump into him on the street from time to time.

Was he really born of a virgin?

[Pause.] Before I answer that you need to give me some good reason why that would matter.

Well, I guess it matters because if he was born of virgin, it would be further evidence that he was really the one, true son of God, as they say.

I know you better than that. You know perfectly well that you don't think about him in such dogmatic terms.

True. But I feel a strong need to ask questions that I think others would think are important, that other people would want answered.

That's fine. It's important to consider others—that's a good enough reason to warrant an answer. But first look at what you're really asking: Here you have a gigantic tree the likes of which the world has never seen, a tree whose branches penetrate every corner of the world. A tree that bears fruit like Mother Teresa and St. Francis of Assisi and Joan of Arc, and you sit there and try to convince me that it matters whether he was born of a virgin because you need further evidence that he was really the son of God. [Laughter.]

Are you going to answer me or not?

Actually, no. You need to figure some things out for yourself.

Was he really crucified? Did he die on the cross and then spring back to life?

Same thing: First tell me why that matters to you.

I can't give you any better reason than I just gave. Some people believe in Jesus in part because they believe he was born of a virgin, was crucified, died for our sins, and was then resurrected.

That is good. They believe, and all is well. This was all foreseen. The whole plan worked beautifully.

Somehow I think you're trying to tell me that it is possible that none of these things occurred in real life.

What do you think? Keep asking yourself why these things matter. They don't. What matters is that you love one another, that you treat your neighbors as you would yourself be treated. For the most part, people who obsess over these flashy historical details tend to lose sight of the real goals.

Here on our plane, the circumstances of Jesus' birth and death seem trivial in the extreme. When the mustard seed was placed into the world, it was placed in such a way that certain stories and certain beliefs would eventually take root in the human psyche.

Whether the events within these stories actually occurred is a matter of profound insignificance. Jesus would be the first to tell you this.

What does matter is his message: Love one another. Think only good of others. Do only good to others.

Jesus lived and died so that a great many people would come to understand that these are the greatest goals: To like others. To love others. To respect others. To accept others and refrain from judgment and superiority. To help others. To get along. To give generously. To keep from harming any other in any way, however subtle. To reach a critical evolutionary endpoint, where you do unto others exactly as you would want them to do unto you, and do this always—with no *exceptions for any reason.*

What matters is that you become a person who helps break the cycles of violence, hatred, and judgment in the world: To turn the other cheek. To stop reacting to violence and ill will with further violence and ill will. These are the things that matter about Jesus. This is why he came: To set into motion an incredibly complex and long-lasting chain of events that would ultimately help you stop hurting yourselves and each other. Others came for the same reason.

[Pause.] Did Jesus really perform the miracles that are described— healing the sick, raising the dead, turning water into wine, and feeding the masses with a few loaves and fishes?

Again: Why do you want to know? You have to have a good reason or I cannot in good conscience give you an answer.

[Pause.] It matters because it would be very beneficial if we could do these things ourselves. If we knew that such miracles were possible, we would know that we might be able to get to the point where we could do them ourselves.

[Softly.] *Now that is a good reason. Yes, he performed the miracles much as they are described in the scriptures. In some places they are exaggerated, and in other places his acts were considerably more impressive than the stories. But by and large, yes, the miracles were real. And yes, you can get to the point where you can do these things yourselves—yet another endpoint of evolution.*

How do we reach this point?

There's only one way: By imitating Christ. By acting like him. By living your life as he did. By loving others as yourselves. By breaking the cycles of violence. By shifting your attention from yourselves to those around you. By giving with great generosity. When you do these things, first in your heart and then in your lives, you will eventually be able to work miracles yourselves. It's very straightforward. In fact, it's so straightforward that it is largely lost upon you.

Are there any rituals or prayers or special techniques Jesus used to enact the miracles?

Not really. The miracles occurred automatically because the way Jesus lived his life set up certain conditions in the space-time continuum around him. In essence, the miracles were performed through love. Love is the ultimate technique, the Philosopher's Stone sought throughout the ages, the magical agent that turns the base into gold, disease into health, ignorance into knowledge, and poverty into abundance.

There were no special spells or mystical rituals used to perform his acts. They occurred spontaneously and usually unconsciously. They occurred in large part as an automatic by-product of his profound concern, affection, and compassion for others. Do not be confused on this issue or you will never learn to do these things yourselves.

Lazarus was raised from the dead because Jesus was so deeply concerned for him and for his family. Lepers, as well as the crippled and the blind, were healed because the surge of compassion that radiated naturally from Jesus when he saw them was so intense and so sincere and so unwavering. The water was turned to wine because he was so joyful at the prospect of the marriage and because he felt such a powerful impulse to express his generosity toward the couple.

[*Pause.*] What was he like? What was he really like?—I mean personality-wise. What was it like to be with him, to talk to him? Are the descriptions in the Bible accurate?

No. The descriptions in the Bible are very sketchy at best and don't even come close to describing what he was really like. He was so much better than you have made him out to be.

He was a very, very kind man and terribly good-natured. He was easygoing, soft-spoken, and infinitely humble—what you would call a "regular guy." He was a great friend and a stupendous companion. He was extremely generous in his affections and in his praise for those around him.

Speaking with him was such a pleasure. He was always turning the conversation back to others, asking about others—their dreams, their plans, their fears, and their loved ones. He held no judgment in his heart for anyone, even criminals. He accepted and liked everyone just as they were, wholeheartedly and without a trace of reservation.

And he was very, very funny. You can't possibly imagine how witty and silly he could be. He could make the people around him laugh so hard and so long that they would beg him to stop. He had an amazing appreciation for the ironic and the absurd. If he lived today he would like The Far Side *and* Seinfeld *very much.*

The Bible conveys little of this. It seems to imply that he took himself very seriously. That he was a very heavy, serious, somber, dignified person—a false image worsened immeasurably by the ridiculous depictions in your motion pictures. I assure you he was nothing of the sort.

Although he could be solemn when the occasion called for it, he was generally quite lighthearted and jubilant. This irritated the authorities to no end. It was they who were weighed down in excessive self-importance and "dignity."

[Pause.] The next question I want to ask concerns a very touchy subject. I've been tiptoeing around this, but I'm going to come right out and ask it point-blank: Was Jesus really the son of God—the one and only son? There is a passage in John that is extremely controversial regarding this. It quotes Jesus as saying, "I am the Way, and the Truth, and the Life. No one comes to the Father but through Me"

(John 14:6 NASB). I've been trying to avoid this question, but I feel that I have to ask it at this time in order to be complete. To leave this out would be less than honest.

The crux of the matter is that many Christians quote this passage as irrefutable evidence that Christianity is the one and only true path. They believe Jesus was saying that all other paths, all other religions, are false and lead to disaster, to eternal damnation for the soul. This passage is at the root of Christianity's condemnation of all other religions and its insistence on converting everyone else to its way of thinking.

First of all, you need to place the quote in context. What does the whole passage really say?

[*Pause.*] Here it is. The quote is from John 14, a passage that describes a conversation Jesus had with his disciples at the end of his life, right before he was arrested and crucified. The sentence was directed specifically at Thomas and reads like this:

Jesus saith unto him, "I am the way, the truth, and the life: No man cometh unto the Father, but by me. If ye had known me, ye should have known my Father also: and from henceforth ye know him, and have seen him." Philip said to him, "Lord, show us the Father, and it sufficeth us." Jesus saith unto him, "Have I been so long a time with you and yet hast thou not known me, Philip? He that hath seen me hath seen the Father; and how sayest thou then, 'Show us the Father?' Believest thou not that I am in the Father, and the Father in me? The words that I speak unto you I speak not of myself: but the Father that dwelleth in me, he doeth the works." (John 14:6–10 KJV)

What you have to understand is that in the Gospels, there are two distinct voices used by Jesus. The first is that of a human being, a man with an ego and a personality like other human beings. The second voice is that of an enlightened being who has realized his oneness with God.

Jesus was near the end of his life when he spoke the words in this passage. That alone should tell you something: That he had reached his peak, that he had become so firmly centered in his enlightenment that his identity as a human being had waned, while his identity as God had waxed to its full intensity. In this state he was no longer a simple man with an ordinary ego, but pure divine consciousness.

When Jesus said "No one comes to the Father but through me" he didn't mean as in "me" the man. He meant, "No one comes to the Father but through this awakening." No one gets to heaven—which he told you was "within"— without attaining this state of consciousness. No one gets to the promised land without realizing his or her oneness with the Source of all being.

Mind you, the other interpretation—the literal or fundamentalist interpretation—is perfectly appropriate for some people and, in a very real sense, just as "true." Remember the mustard seed principle: Jesus was a man placed into the world in such a way that the stories, texts, and interpretations that would inevitably follow him would have meaning for everyone in every stage of personal evolution.

So when some Christians say that all Jews, and Buddhists, and Hindus, and pagans are doomed to an afterlife in hell because they don't accept Christ as their personal savior, they are totally incorrect, I hope?

[Laughter.] *Come on. You have never bought into that preposterous notion. Jesus was himself a Jew. How could he say that all Jews were doomed to eternal hell? That doesn't make any sense at all. There are many paths to God.*

I need to ask because other people will want to hear your opinion on the subject. Let me ask you another question that is related to this issue. You keep talking about "stages" of "personal evolution." Are you trying to imply that fundamentalists with their literal interpretations of the Bible are somehow at a "lower" level of evolution than other more progressive individuals who adhere to metaphysical and metaphorical interpretations? That seems very judgmental.

No. Of course not. One level of human thought is not "better" or "higher" than another, per se. God is like the hub of a great wheel. The paths all creatures take to reach the center are like the spokes of the wheel. Different people simply come at God from different directions.

There are many ways to reach the final goal, and none is necessarily better than another. Each path is perfectly suited for a certain kind of person. But make no mistake, all paths converge at one final doorway. At that door there must be a full realization that the self is one and the same as God or the final threshold cannot be passed. In the end, the ego must dissolve, as Jesus' ego dissolved, and the true self must open fully to accept its pure divinity. No one comes to the One but through this realization.

All of the world's religions are perfectly valid and of equal importance in the mind of God. Each was created as a vehicle to deliver a certain kind of person to the final realization. If you look at each of these paths carefully, taking care to see through the confusion that different languages and cultures create, you will find that each contains at its center an enlightened individual, a person who realized his or her own true identity as the One. Jesus was indeed the son of God, there is no doubt about it. But so was Buddha, and Mohammed, and all the rest. Every being is on an appropriate road to the One, and everyone will arrive safely in the end.

Chapter Eleven

In most hospitals, the only physician physically present after hours is the ER doctor. For this reason, it is his or her responsibility to pronounce death for nearly all patients who expire in the middle of the night. There are many.

Mrs. Laramie had been dying very slowly for the last two weeks. A massive stroke had taken everything but the part of her brain that controlled basic functions such as breathing. She had left strict instructions that no extraordinary measures be taken if something like this happened.

Just before dawn one summer night, the nurses called me up to the medical floor to do my duty. Mrs. Laramie was lying there staring into space with half-closed eyes, her mouth open slightly. I went through the motions, listening to her heart, trying to find a pulse, then closed her eyes and folded her hands.

Still half asleep, I thought I caught a glimmer of something in the corner of my eye, as though the air in the corner had shifted slightly.

Are you there?
You know better. We're always here.

Always?

Always. We're all over the hospital all the time.

Is she all right? I can't sense her somehow.

She was gone a long time ago and her angels with her.

So you're...

I'm here for you.

[*Silence.*] There are some things I have been wanting to ask you about but have been avoiding.

[Laughter.] *Here you go again. It's amazing how squeamish you can be about these things. Look, I'll say it for you and get it out of the way: Money!* [Peals of laughter.] *Money, money, money!*

[*Cringing.*] You don't have to yell. That word just sounds so... sacrilegious, especially coming from you.

[Laughter.] *I know. Almost all of you are the same way. You're totally obsessed with money but you tiptoe around the subject the same way you tiptoe around sex. You're secretive and embarrassed about a perfectly natural part of life.*

I have trouble seeing how money is a "natural" phenomenon. It is clearly manmade and seems to cause a lot of problems for people.

Really? What do you think money actually is?

Simple. It is an artificial commodity that has been created so that goods and services can be traded and transferred in a convenient manner.

I see. Goods and services. And what, may I ask, are goods and services?

That's a very vague question. Can you be more specific?

[Laughing.] *No. The question is perfectly clear.*

Okay. Goods and services are products that human beings create that have value.

Pick an example—any example.

How about a bushel of corn.

Fine. How is a bushel of corn created?

A farmer prepares his field, plants some seed corn, cultivates and fertilizes the plants as they emerge, harvests the yield, and transports the resultant crop to the marketplace.

Sounds like a lot of work.

It is a lot of work. Generally speaking, it takes a lot of work to make money.

Sometimes. So, explain to me what work is.

A lot of intense time and energy.

Keep going. You'll get there. What is time?

You know what time is, what kind of a question is that?

The question is, do you really know what time is.

[Silence.] No, not really. I'm not entirely sure even physicists really know what time is. [Pause.] I thought you said it was the process of cause and effect playing out on the material plane.

What is time for you?

For me, a segment of time is a segment of my life, a slice of the allotted interval I have been granted to exist here on Earth.

Very good. Would you agree, then, that time is, in essence, life?

I suppose you could say that, yes.

Can you think of any commodity or any service that is not the direct result of someone spending a segment of their very life to produce?

How about gold? Gold has been the basis of many monetary systems. It is created by nature.

Yes, it is created by nature, that's true. But how do you acquire some?

Okay, you've got me there. Somebody has to prospect for it, then mine it, refine it, transport it, etc., etc.

Human beings have had to expend a portion of their lives to obtain it, right?

Yes, they have had to expend time and energy.

[Pause.] *So let me ask you again. What is money?*

Money is a symbol that represents life?

Excellent! Now, why should that be shameful in any way, shape, or form. Is life shameful?

No, of course not.

Then get over it. Money is a perfectly natural part of your life. There is nothing wrong with it.

What then of the love or "lust" of money? It is said that the obsession with money is the "root of all evil."

There is truth in that statement. But you have to understand what it really means. The lust of money is a misguided state of consciousness, a state of misunderstanding. When people lust after money they are going after the symbol itself without understanding that the money is really life. This disconnect causes all kinds of problems. When money is seen as a kind of inanimate commodity and not the life force of other people, then all kinds of mischief can be justified to obtain it. Can you see that?

Possibly. [*Pause.*] Yes, I suppose I can see how that is true.

A person who really understands—at a deep, visceral level—that money is a symbol for the hopes, dreams, sweat, attention, and love of other human beings will be powerfully motivated to handle money with extreme care and consideration of those human beings. Unless they don't mind if a lot of unfortunate things happen for them.

You lost me there for a second. I can see how money is a symbol for human time and energy, but I'm not sure how it symbolizes love.

Go back to the farmer. He expends a lot of time and effort and attention to produce his bushel of corn, right?

Yes.

You just have to keep tracing things back to their source. Why does the farmer produce the bushel of corn? You grew up in farm country, this shouldn't be too hard for you. Think of a specific farmer you knew. Why was he producing his corn?

The one I am thinking of produced corn so that he could provide for his family, I suppose.

Good. And why did he…

Okay. I can see it. Obviously, he loved his family.

Is it difficult to see how the corn, then, is ultimately a product of his love?

No. That conclusion seems fairly supportable.

[Laughter.] *Do you think that love is somehow the root of all evil?*

No, that's silly. Besides, there is no evil. I've been convinced of that.

Then isn't it okay to love money? Isn't loving money loving love itself? Is that not a worthy state of consciousness? Assuming, of course, that such a love takes place while thoroughly understanding that money is really a symbol for the sweat and dreams of human beings.

I can see how it would be okay to love money in this way.

Good. Because you can only really get to the place where money is effortless if you attain this state of consciousness. Money will not flow freely into your life until you have dropped all your hang-ups about it. Only when you have resolved your subtle sense of shame and guilt will your subconscious blocks fall away. Only then will you feel that it is entirely acceptable for you to create money and succeed in doing so.

Create money?

We've been through this before. You know perfectly well that you create the world around you. And that obviously includes money. In fact, it especially includes money. As much as you hate to admit it with all your subtle hang-ups, money is a huge part of your life—of everyone's life. As such, it represents a huge portion of your creative energy. Your financial state of affairs is a direct reflection of an enormous fraction of your overall thought processes.

Money is not a huge part of *everyone's* life. A lot of people get by on very little and turn their attention to other matters—high, spiritual matters.

Nonsense. If you look at nearly all of those people you will find that they expend a large amount of their time and energy obtaining all the various forms of supply necessary to sustain growth and happiness. And every one of those forms of supply is linked in some way to money. All of the forms of energy in your lives are linked in an enormous web, a kind of ecological system. Money is the matrix of that web.

What about someone like Mother Teresa? She wasn't that concerned with money. Almost all of her energy was devoted to higher things. Shouldn't we strive to be like her?

[Laughter.] *That's so naive. Mother Teresa was obsessed with helping others. The people she served were extraordinarily poor. One of the most important things she did was to find supply for these unfortunate individuals. If you really look at her life you can see that she was actually like a gigantic conduit through which supply, including vast quantities of money, flowed.*

Mother Teresa was directly responsible for attracting millions of dollars in donations to the Church. She spent much of her life turning these donations into food, shelter, and medical supplies and channeling them to the right recipients.

What should really interest you right now is the way you are struggling to make a case that there is something wrong with money. Look at yourself. You really have quite an investment in your subconscious hang-ups, don't you?

How am I supposed to get rid of these?

Like any other problem, your problem with money must first be solved at the level of consciousness. Be increasingly and ever vigilant of the real significance of money. Constantly strive to see it as a symbol of life and love. Over and over and over practice this. Work at it. Pay attention.

It will take time, but if you persist you will eventually come to believe—at the deepest possible subconscious level—that money is a wonderful and beautiful thing. When this happens, you will feel free to create money and it will begin to move with ever-increasing fluidity through your life.

But take care. Notice that I said through *your life. I didn't say it should or would flow* into *your life. There is a big difference.*

How so? I mean, I think I know where you are going with this, but I want to be very clear on the matter.

Good. Because this is even more important than removing shame. You have to spend the money that flows into your life properly. Most important, you need to give a good portion of it away. If you fail in this matter you will continue to experience lack.

Give plenty of money away. Give it away regularly and give it away carefully. Don't just give it blindly to any charity. Do your homework and make sure it goes where it will be used efficiently. Slow down and pay attention for a few hours each month studying your options. And when you see something on the news, about a tragedy or a disaster, do something. Pick up the phone and donate.

And don't count money you channel to any organization with any kind of political agenda, even if that is a religious organization. Such organizations are almost invariably tainted with peculiar and selfish motives. You can give to them if you want, but don't expect such gifts to help your own state of flow.

People should give other things too. Give your time. Give your attention. Give this book away. Give your old things away. All of these things will help you.

Give anonymously whenever possible and give to organizations and individuals that won't give you any significant recognition. Unless you are highly experienced in such matters, recognition will tend to fuel your ego, your sense of self-importance. This in turn will stem the flow. And whatever you do, be constantly grateful for what you have and use it to its maximum.

Practice these things consistently and carefully and you will experience perfect abundance.

There has to be more to it than that. What else can you tell me about this?

Actually, I think I'm going to pass. You know what you people say: "Keep it simple, stupid." You can get more involved in the next book.

The next book? I have to do this again?

[Laughter.] You'll choose to do this again and when you do we can get into much greater detail. For now you need to master the basics. Here's the

program for mastering money and achieving abundance—don't make it any more complicated than this.

First, think good and loving thoughts about money. Every single time you handle money, trace it in your mind to its source. Become as conscious as possible that when you are handling money, you are handling a human being's life along with that person's hopes, dreams, loves, and losses. When you are handling large sums, realize that you are handling the lives of many human beings. Be careful. Respect money and honor it for what it is. As you practice these things, your shame and your fear surrounding money and other critical forms of supply will begin to fall away. Then your subconscious mind will give you the green light to create an abundant flow.

Second, visualize abundant supply coming to you and see yourself using it for the greater good. Form follows thought. Prepare the channel in your mind and the substance will follow.

Third, be constantly and deeply grateful for everything you have now. Be an excellent steward of the resources with which you have been entrusted. Use what you have to the maximum and with great care.

Fourth—and most important—watch your outflow. This includes being highly responsible about money you owe to others for their time and effort. Release money generously and regularly. Give, give, and give again. Recycle everything. More people fail in this area than any other.

Anyone seeking to solve the flow of money must practice these principles faithfully and with great persistence until they are absolutely automatic.

Although poorly understood, the parable of the talents addressed this. The servants who had learned their lessons well were told: "You have been faithful over a few things, I will make you ruler over many things" (Matthew 25:23 NKJV). Perfect these basic attitudes and practices, and I promise you will be given more to work with.

The Universe watches you, monitors you. When it sees that you are reliable, that you can be trusted to handle the current correctly, it will gradually channel more in your direction.

Chapter Twelve

The situation that enabled communication in this instance was very brief. As I was soon to find, there was a reason for this.

A man was brought from the nursing home who had been dead for over an hour. He had been near death for weeks and had died peacefully in his sleep. I went through the usual motions and pronounced him dead at 2 a.m. Completely exhausted, I shuffled back to my room. But I couldn't sleep and went to work at my laptop.

People who have looked over the preceding chapters have been asking me a lot of questions about the material that has been presented. One of the most frequent questions has to do with the way these conversations take place. People really want to know if it is possible for them to speak with the Spirit and, if so, how to go about it.

As they should. It is your destiny as a people to learn to speak with us through the veil. In time, every one of you will do this.

Several years ago I read this interesting book called *The Origin of Consciousness in the Breakdown of the Bicameral Mind* by a Princeton psychologist named Julian Jaynes. This book presents a fascinating

theory. The author constructs a very scholarly and compelling case
that up until two or three thousand years ago, many human beings
were in a constant, subtle state of hallucination. In this state of
mind, people thought they were communing with various aspects
of a spirit world. I could be wrong, but the author strikes me as
either an atheist or someone who otherwise thinks that the world of
spirit is a delusion concocted by the mind.

[Laughter.] *Actually, the author sounds like a very perceptive person. He
got the time frame just about right, but he made one critical mistake: People
weren't hallucinating. Back in those days most people actually did perceive and
commune with the spirit world.*

So what happened? What went wrong? Why did we all lose this
ability?

*Religion happened. That's what went wrong. A class of people arose who
began to make their living mediating between God and normal people. They
quickly found this was big business—very, very big business.*

*For thousands of years the shaman, medicine woman, priest, and priestess
have been revered. Great status has been conferred on those who are thought to
hold the keys to the world of spirit. Consequently, the priestly class has had an
incredibly strong motivation to keep everyone else from talking directly to God. If
people were to remember that they were able to speak directly to God without an
intermediary, the holy men and women and all of their highly profitable institu-
tions would be put out of business in short order.*

*For the most part this has all taken place at a subtle, subliminal level. Priests
and churches haven't set about to separate people from their God in a conscious
and deliberate manner. Religion has been an honorable and virtuous institution
for the most part. But the individuals who populate its hierarchies are subject to
the usual frailties of human nature. They have survival instincts like everyone
else. In their fear they have produced within the societies they serve a distinct
sense of fear and shame about speaking with us directly.*

In the Middle Ages, when the Church was an extremely powerful, profit-able, and corrupt political entity, this fear and shame were overt. In essence, the Inquisition was a direct manifestation of the Church's desire to keep people from hearing the Spirit directly. In those years you could be labeled as a witch or heretic and be burned at the stake for speaking directly with us. Consider Joan of Arc.

The most abusive mechanisms which have been used to keep people from communing directly with God have long since been abolished. But this has only made room for more acceptable—but equally effective—psychological devices.

Let me ask you this: In your experience, how do people who belong to an organized religion tend to receive the information in this book and others like it?

Generally speaking, they act like it's not okay for me to speak with you. It's acceptable for saints and mystics who have received some type of certified seal of approval to speak with Spirit and to have other transcendent experiences, but it's really not at all accept-able for your average Joe like me to undertake this. It's considered sacrilegious. A common reaction is: "Who do you think you are to have taken this upon yourself? Who are you to believe you can do this? How shameful!"

[Laughter.] *I can tell you without a doubt that it is all right. It's fine for you, it's fine for all your friends, all your family, all your coworkers, and for everyone else in your society to make their own direct spiritual connection. The fear and guilt that are present in your society regarding this will fall away in time.*

When this happens you will all return to the state you were in thousands of years ago and you will all hear us and even see us. With one big difference: Next time around you will be able to appreciate the experience.

Long ago, you took your ability to hear God for granted. As your saying goes: "You don't know what you've got till it's gone." When the ability is finally returned to you—or, more correctly, when you take it back—you will cherish and protect it as the greatest of gifts.

[*Pause.*] How should we go about taking this ability back? Where do we start? How should the average person begin?

You have to start by just doing it. There is no substitute for action. You have to practice. You have to start somewhere. Do you remember how you began?

Yes. I had the audacity to simply assume that I could and should try. But then again, I had a lot of help. I was fortunate enough to be a physician and to be present when people were dying. Normal people don't have this advantage.

Actually, your ability to speak with us had very little to do with the fact that you were around dying people. We are present all around you—all of you—all the time. We're perfectly willing to speak with anyone under any circumstances, unusual or otherwise.

So that's all in my head—that you are only present when people are dying, that the death of my patients is somehow necessary for me to communicate with you?

Yes. It's just a crutch. But it worked well enough. It got you started and thus served a very useful purpose. But it's time to let this fall away and proceed to the next level.

So what you're telling me is that I can sit down and write this stuff anytime? You're saying that *anyone* can do this anytime?

I've been trying to make this clear repeatedly.

But how are we supposed to get in the right state of mind? The usual chaotic state of mind of everyday life is not conducive to spiritual conversations. It can't be, or I would be talking to you all the time.

Oh, you can get to the place where you talk to us all the time, even when you are engaged in complex and stressful worldly activities. But for now, your question is well taken. There are some things you can do to get into a state of consciousness that facilitates things nicely.

We need to know about this.

The best technique known is what you refer to as meditation.

What kind of meditation? There are a lot of different kinds.

Nearly any type of meditation will suffice provided it is practiced correctly and consistently. There are Christian meditations, Buddhist meditations, Hindu and Muslim meditations, Native American meditations, and many others. They all work beautifully if they are practiced properly.

That's too general. Give us something specific.

Okay. You know that part of the Lord's Prayer that says "hallowed be thy name"?

Sure. Everybody knows that.

What do you think that means?

It's just a kind of general statement of respect and adulation that gets the prayer off to a good start, I suppose.

Are you sure about that? What does the whole sentence say?

"Our Father who art in heaven, hallowed be thy name."

And where is heaven?

Within. That much is clear.

Now here's the big question: What is God's name?

He has many, many names.

True. And they are all accurate. But what is his name in the Judeo-Christian tradition?

[Pause.] Jehovah?

Go back further. What is the name, the most ancient, the most sacred name for God in the Judeo-Christian tradition?

Yahweh?

It's pronounced Yeahvay. This is the "name" that is referred to in the Lord's Prayer. This is the name of God that is said to be so sacred that it is never to be uttered aloud.

Here is one of the most powerful and wonderful secrets you can ever know in all your life and it is my pleasure to give it to you and all that read this book: If

you dwell on this name in your mind over and over, day after day, month after
month, all good things will come to you. As it is said, "Your Father knows what
things you have need of even before you ask" (Matthew 6:86 NKJV).

You mean we should repeat this name over and over—like a mantra? I thought that was forbidden. Let me look this up for a minute.
[*Pause.*] Here it is in Matthew 6. Right before Jesus gives the Lord's
Prayer he says, "When ye pray, use not vain repetitions, as the hea-
then do: For they think that they shall be heard for their much speaking" (Matthew 6:7 KJV).

There are two things to remember when repeating the name of God. Do not
do it vainly. This means that you do not do it in an empty, mechanical manner.
This is disrespectful and wholly ineffective.

The second thing to remember is to repeat the name silently within. Heaven
is within. You don't blab it loudly all over the place thinking that this will get you
extra points. Go back up a verse and read what it says.

"When you pray, enter into your closet, and when you have
shut the door, pray to your Father which is in secret: and your
Father who sees in secret will reward you openly."

So *how* exactly do you repeat the name of God? You just say it
over and over silently and respectfully?

Pretty much, yes. But there are some refinements in this regard that are very help-
ful. First of all, you have to understand that one of the primary benefits of repeating
the name of God is that it gets you to stop thinking. Your incessant stream of internal
dialogue is the main thing that keeps you from hearing the voice of the Spirit.

When you repeat the name of GOD you want to capitalize on this fact and
do it in such a way that your thoughts are gradually lengthened and slowed.

How is this done exactly?

Each syllable should be repeated rather slowly. Start by taking about a sec-

ond each to sound "Yah" and "Vay." After a few minutes lengthen each to about two seconds, and eventually three and four. There should be a little rest between each syllable and each repetition. You'll just have to do it to see what I mean. The sounds will resonate at a certain frequency. You'll know what frequency is best when you actually start doing it: It feels good when you hit the right pitch and the right speed.

To further enhance the benefits of this meditation you can work with your breathing. "Yah" should be on the inhalation and "Vay" on the exhalation. The breath should come and go in a very smooth, peaceful, leisurely fashion. You should watch the breath "fall" in and out of your body effortlessly.

Finally, focus on your heart as you do this. Visualize and feel the sounds, along with your breath, flowing in and out of your heart.

What will happen if this meditation is practiced regularly? Are there any specific benefits?

Everything *is* corrected. The meditation balances everything in your life. You will achieve harmony with all those around you. This harmony will bring you respect and love and understanding from others. Your flow of supply on all levels will gradually improve. Your health will improve. Your intellect will improve. As I said, everything will improve.

[Pause.] *Let me ask you something I think is important. What do you think evolution is? What happens when someone "evolves"?*

I've always thought the main thing to remember is that evolution is much different than "growth." Growth is simply the process of getting bigger or better while remaining essentially the same being. For example, an apple tree can grow to be very large but is still an apple tree—it hasn't evolved.

By contrast, evolution is the process of completely dying to yourself and reawakening in an entirely new form. Evolution is a quantum leap, a jump to a completely new and higher level of being.

Do the two processes feel different?

Usually, yes. Getting bigger and better during a growth phase can often feel really good. Dying to yourself can often be extremely painful. In many instances, death of the self is brought about by a terrible tragedy. A broken heart, the death of a child or spouse, a life-threatening disease, a state of extreme peril or poverty—these are the kinds of experiences that often throw one over the edge and into an evolutionary spiral.

But there's more to how evolution feels. Recovering from such an experience, reawakening in a new life after such a tragedy, can be ecstatic. Landing on the other side in a shining new form after a particularly daunting leap of faith through the darkness can be a phenomenal experience.

Is that why you refer to yourself as a messenger of evolution and not as a messenger of death?

Yes. [Pause.] *I wanted to know if you understood these basic points before I told you the following: The fact is that meditating on Yahweh as the name of God has a powerful effect on evolution—it accelerates it greatly. When you engage in the Yahweh meditation regularly and correctly, all sorts of amazing and unexpected things start to happen in your life. You start developing in ways you never thought possible and at a rate that is astonishing.*

But the really terrific part is that you do so with less pain. Evolution can actually proceed in a smooth, orderly, and pleasurable way when it is approached correctly. Concentration on this sound balances everything—your family life, your love life, your financial life, and your career are all synchronized. Everything is adjusted and integrated and starts to fire on all eight cylinders. And that feels great.

I'm telling you, the power in this secret is beyond your current comprehension. Do not take any of this lightly or attempt to play with it like a toy. Be sober, quiet, and careful in your practice so you don't unleash too much energy too quickly. If you do, you might evolve more quickly than you care to.

Let me ask you something else: Do you know where the name Yahweh originated?

It is my understanding that the ancient Jews used to write the name of God with what is known as the Tetragrammaton because it was too sacred, too powerful to speak. All this means is that they wrote the name as four Hebrew consonants. These are variously transliterated as YHWH, YHVH, JHVH, or IHVH. They left the vowels out so that even when they wrote the name of God they wouldn't refer openly to the actual sound of the name. They felt it was far too powerful for most people to know without proper preparation. I think this happened about 300 B.C. At this point in history they started to substitute the less direct names of Adonai or Elohim when referring to God in conversation.

It's interesting, isn't it? That was right about the time people stopped communing with the Spirit, according to the book you quoted earlier. This ancient name with roots so deep they touch the very source of the entire Judeo-Christian phenomenon—we now turn to this and find an extraordinarily potent key to contemporary evolution. [Laughter.] Sometimes you have to go all the way back to the beginning in order to evolve.

[Pause.] When you practice the Yahweh meditation, your ability to commune with Spirit will improve. When you still your own thoughts, the thoughts of God, who is within, will become evident.

In this state you will be able to converse with God and any of his manifestations—any of his agents or "messengers"—if you will only try.

But you have to try. You have to speak to us and you have to listen. And you have to trust what you are hearing.

Use your imagination. Get into the right state of mind, ask what you want, then imagine what the reply is. Don't be afraid and don't lock up. Be creative. Remember that your imagination, the part of your mind that can form images, is a divine faculty. Trust it.

And don't worry about whether your conversations are acceptable to anyone else. Don't ask for anyone else's permission or blessing. That is always a big mistake. No human being, no religious official, no family member, no friend—no one has the authority to give or deny permission for you to speak with God. In fact, most people should strenuously avoid telling anyone else about their conversations. Your relationship with Spirit is no one else's business.

[Pause.] There's so much more I want to know.

In good time. Think about all the things I have told you. Practice. Put these suggestions to work in your life.

After a time, we will speak again. [Laughter.] When that day comes, you will not need to be at work and no one will have to die for us to speak.

About the Author

Todd Michael, D.O., served as the medical director of an emergency room and level-three trauma center while writing *The Evolution Angel*. He has attended the deaths of more than five hundred patients in his career. He is board-certified in family practice and maintains additional certification in advanced trauma life support and advanced cardiac life support. Michael, whose undergraduate degree is in psychology, was accepted into the Mensa society in 1985.

Michael lives in Boulder, Colorado, where he writes and works as a life coach; he travels widely as a motivational speaker. The author of five books, including *The Twelve Conditions of a Miracle* and *The Hidden Parables*, both published by Tarcher/Penguin, he previously used the pen name Michael Abrams to protect his patients and personal life. He is also an accomplished painter and recording artist working from Essene Studios.

Michael sponsors several Native American and Third World children and supports Doctors Without Borders and other international rescue groups. He is also an avid supporter of Amnesty International and a variety of environmental causes.